Unfolding The Lotus

Unfolding The Lotus

Spirit Reflections on Mediumship

Paul and Eileen McGlone

iUniverse, Inc.
New York Lincoln Shanghai

Unfolding The Lotus
Spirit Reflections on Mediumship

Copyright © 2005 by Paul and Eileen McGlone

All rights reserved. No part of this book may be used or reproduced by any means, graphic, electronic, or mechanical, including photocopying, recording, taping or by any information storage retrieval system without the written permission of the publisher except in the case of brief quotations embodied in critical articles and reviews.

iUniverse books may be ordered through booksellers or by contacting:

iUniverse
2021 Pine Lake Road, Suite 100
Lincoln, NE 68512
www.iuniverse.com
1-800-Authors (1-800-288-4677)

The moral rights of the authors have been asserted.

A catalogue record for this book is available from the British Library.

ISBN-13: 978-0-595-37989-7 (pbk)
ISBN-13: 978-0-595-82360-4 (ebk)
ISBN-10: 0-595-37989-3 (pbk)
ISBN-10: 0-595-82360-2 (ebk)

Printed in the United States of America

To our Home Circle

And all participants of our Meditation and
Development Groups

Hai's Message

'Walk forward with hope'

Hai was asked whether he had a title in mind for this book. He answered:

'Unfolding the Lotus' because the lotus is a beautiful flower. However when the petals of the lotus are closed you cannot see its inner beauty, but as the petals of the lotus unfold you see its beauty in all its glory. And it is a bit like that with your development, with the development of your 'third eye'.

Before you know anything about your 'third eye' it is just a total mystery to you but then you get flashes of insight and you start to acknowledge its existence, its reality and its purpose and you start to see the glimmerings of its beauty. As you practise and develop and as your skill becomes more refined, you see this lotus manifest as it opens itself out to you, to your full view, and you may see its glory in all its beauty.

Therefore, 'Unfolding the Lotus' is a title that we are happy with, for the centre of the lotus is unknown to those who have not seen it, but to those whom it has opened itself out to; it can be seen in all its radiant beauty.

The contents of this book are offered in good faith, and we have accepted the identity of the spirits given to us. However, Hai has often warned us about the difficulties of communication between the spirit and earth realms. Therefore, in this as in other things, Hai would commend to you a saying:

"Test all things. If in your heart you feel them true and correct then hold to them. If not, discard them. This is why you were given your minds, to question not to follow blindly as some do, unfortunately."

Contents

The Phoenix Group xv

Eileen's Note xvii

Introduction xix

PART 1   *Mediumship Basics*

Chapter 1   Principles & Process of Communication 3
Chapter 2   Influence of Guides & Helpers 25
Chapter 3   Ethics & Responsibilities of Mediumship 37
Chapter 4   Difficulties of Communication 42
Chapter 5   Thomas: Communication & Protection 49
Chapter 6   A Private Sitting 52

PART 2   *Exercises for Development*

Chapter 7   Chan Chou: Cupped Hands &
               Blank Screen Exercises 59
Chapter 8   Jacob Session 1: Purpose of Mediumship 65
Chapter 9   Jacob Session 2: Different Forms of
               Communication 75
Chapter 10   Jacob Session 3: Problems During
               Communication 82
Chapter 11   Jacob Session 4: Giving Messages 87
Chapter 12   Jacob Session 5: Interpretation of Symbolism 94
Chapter 13   Jacob Session 6: Philosophy Night 101
Chapter 14   Jacob Session 7: The Need for Practise 112

Chapter 15	Jacob Session 8: More about Contacting Guides	115
Chapter 16	Jacob's Workshop	120
Chapter 17	Hai & Jonathan: Exercises & Interpreting Images	140

PART 3	*Meditation & Its Value*	
Chapter 18	Development through Meditation	153
Chapter 19	Isleen: How to Understand & Use Images in Medtiation	157
Chapter 20	A Selection of Meditations	162

PART 4	*A Selection of Spirit Guest Speakers*	
Chapter 21	James: 'Guides & Other Things'	173
Chapter 22	WB: 'The Orchestrator'	178
Chapter 23	Ada: 'A Light Interlude'	180
Chapter 24	Carol: 'Spirit Connection'	184
Chapter 25	Joseph: 'Why Spirits Communicate'	187

PART 5	*The Development of Trance Mediumship*	
Chapter 26	The Process of Trance	193
Chapter 27	Isleen: The Difficulties of Trance	203

PART 6	*Physical Mediumship/Phenomena*	
Chapter 28	Questions on Physical Mediumship/Phenomena	209
Chapter 29	Tools to help Physical Phenomena	215
Chapter 30	WB: Talking about Physical Phenomena	223
Chapter 31	Jon: Lighting	232
Chapter 32	Lennox: Get the Music Right	234
Chapter 33	Jonathan: The Scientist	236

Chapter 34	Harold: Energy Changes 238
Chapter 35	Jacob & Bill: More about Energies 239
Chapter 36	Jonah: The Governing Council 241
Chapter 37	Stevenson: Evidence 245

PART 7	*General Questions & More about the Phoenix Group*
Chapter 38	General Questions 251
Chapter 39	More about the Phoenix Group....................................256

About the Authors 265

The Phoenix Spirit Group

Below are some of the communicators who are featured throughout this book. You will find other information about them throughout the book and in the last chapter, 'Some Light-hearted Fun,' we tell you a little more about each of the regular members of our Spirit Group.

Hai (pronounced Hay)
Hai is the leader of the Phoenix group and is clearly an evolved soul. His reason for communicating with us is to pass on wisdom and teaching. In this book Hai answers many questions about communicating with spirit as well as the ethics and responsibility of mediumship.

WB (first name William but prefers WB)
WB is our spirit scientist who works with the energies of the group during our sittings. WB advises on all matters of the metaphysical. Some of WB's communications can sound a little formal; however, as you read through the book you will come to know him a little better and appreciate the lighter side of his personality.

Davia (not his real name but tells us he likes the sound Davia, with the emphasis on the last a)
Davia is the Phoenix Group's manager/gatekeeper. He vets and organises all the 'guest spirits' and facilitates their communication through Paul. Davia's second role is to lighten the energies and this the reader will find evident as the book unfolds. When a member of our group (earth side) becomes too serious and the energies heavy, he will often put in his two-pennyworth by passing on his light-hearted banter and jokes through whomever spirit happens to be talking to us at the time. This can often be distracting to the poor spirit who is attempting to communicate with us; nevertheless, it does without doubt have the effect of lightening the energies.

Jacob

Jacob is not one of the original members of the Phoenix group but was chosen by them and so 'co-opted on' later. He has been with the Spirit Group for some years now and regularly takes our Home Circle and development groups through our paces in the development of mediumship. A large section of this book is devoted to the lectures and exercises that Jacob has offered us over the years. You can read more about Jacob in many other parts of this book.

Isleen

Isleen, you might say, was one of the founder members of the Phoenix group. She is a lovely gentle soul who takes us through our weekly meditations. You will find more of Isleen's communications throughout this book and you can read a selection of her meditations in Part Three.

Eileen's Note

Jacob
The Lead Player

Our 'Stage Manager,' Davia, has often told us, with great exuberance, that we have 'a cast of thousands,' working to help us in this enterprise, and we have little doubt that there are many, many more spirits, other than those we speak to, who work away in the background, doing their bit to help. So it would be wrong to single out any one spirit and say that he or she had contributed more to the endeavour. Nevertheless, as you will see when you read further into this book, Hai has indicated that it took the Phoenix Group some time before they found someone suitable to lead us in our development sessions. It would seem that the Spirit Group 'auditioned,' those spirits who were interested, for the 'part;' though they might not describe it quite like that. Therefore, in choosing Jacob, they actually cast him as the 'lead player.' For the reasons given above, it probably wouldn't be right for us to name Jacob the 'star' of the enterprise; however, we believe it is important to acknowledge Jacob's contribution, for without him, who knows, this book may never have been written.

*   *   *

One night, one member of our group asked Jacob what he thought about our decision to write a book, based upon his workshops. As you will see from his response below, he was quite excited by the prospect.

Jacob told us:

Yes, I'm pleased with this. I will help you; we can do it. We can do all kinds of things with this book. We could do some exercises; we could do some meditations, some transcripts of a development session. We could do some sort of talking, lectures, yes, on the issues, the principles, the difficulties, the approaches. Chung Ching (another spirit who communicates from time to time) will have his hands full. He helps from afar.

Paul had 'received' an image for the book cover and a title. Someone asked:

Did you or Hai send Paul the message about the title and image, for the cover of the new book?

Jacob replied:
Yes, we did discuss this. It is a possible useful title, 'Unfolding the Lotus' to symbolise development, because it is a process of unfoldment. It is a gradual process, like the petals of the lotus slowly, gently, open and this is the way to do it in development, slowly, confidently, patiently and with interest.

Introduction

By Paul McGlone

In our first book, 'Spirits Speaking from the Heart,' published in 2003, we tried to give the overall flavour of the spirit communications that we'd received through our connection with the Phoenix Spirit Group. In the present book we have decided to focus upon communications relating to the development of mediumship and awareness of spirit energies.

This subject is one that is dear to the hearts of many members of our Home Circle. Indeed it is because of this and other interests expressed by them, that the work with our Spirit Group has evolved in certain directions. Several years ago now, one member of our Home Circle asked Hai about the possibility of the Spirit Group providing meditations to aid our development. Hai responded to this request and so was born the regular meditations that, in the main, Isleen took the lead in providing. We have since been astounded by the variety of meditations, which Isleen has given us and as examples, we have included two of them in this book. We've also included extracts from some of the discussions that followed these meditations and which at times, have focussed upon issues of interpreting images and symbols.

Hai has always said that regular meditation is the foundation upon which other development rests and it was fitting that the meditations were the first extension of our work with the Spirit Group. After many months of piloting with our Home Circle, the Spirit Group indicated their readiness to make the meditations available to a wider audience, and so was born our regular Meditation Evenings that have now been in existence for several years.

The next development came when another member of the Home Circle asked Hai if the Spirit Group would be able to specifically facilitate the development of spirit awareness and communication i.e. mediumship. Hai again responded to the request and consequently we had visits from a number of new spirits who had evidently been given the task of assisting us in this. Each of these spirit people was interesting and we learnt something from their different approaches. However, we soon realised that the Spirit Group were experimenting, trying to find a spirit for the task who would be the 'best fit' with our group. We were eventually introduced to Jacob, a spirit who told us he was a Jewish watchmaker in Poland about two hundred years ago. We quickly took to Jacob with his affable manner, ready conversation, and gentle sense of humour. It was made clear that Jacob was here to stay.

After another phase of piloting within our Home Circle, the Spirit Group again indicated that we should offer the experience to a wider audience and so was created our, for want of a better term, 'Mediumship/Psychic Development' evenings.

Much of the content of this book dates from the time when Jacob first started to work with us. Hai supplied us with the title of this book, 'Unfolding the Lotus.' We added the subtitle 'Spirit Reflections on Mediumship' as this; we feel reflects the format of the book. This book is not designed to be a manual on how to develop mediumship; rather, it is spirit communications about mediumship, in which they give us a series of insights and pointers on how to approach development and issues, which commonly arise. In spite of the difficulties, the view of the Spirit Group is that most of us can be mediumistic to a greater or lesser degree, with practise. The key requirement is to be open to the possibility; following this, it is down to consistent, regular practise.

The book commences with discussions with Hai and some of the other spirits about some of the key issues regarding communication, the process, and its difficulties. Many issues are discussed here, such as; protection, the role of guides, the interpretation of images and symbols, dangers of prediction, the degree of accuracy in communication and 'contamination' by the medium's mind. Many of these questions and discussions reflect the nature of the concerns of members of our Home Circle and others who were engaged in developing their mediumship.

It has been evident that people attending our awareness groups can have different motivations and purposes in seeking development. Some have been keen to develop mediumship in one of its forms, whilst others have focussed more on their own self-awareness and spiritual development. Yet others have been keen to develop as vehicles for healing. Jacob has always been quick to recognise people's varying motivations and to support this. He has also regularly stressed that we are all individuals and the pattern of our development may vary. Therefore, while we may learn much from the experiences of others, our own pattern of development may well vary from theirs. So, we should be careful not to limit or constrain ourselves by attempting to fit into someone else's mould and so create rigid expectations for our own development.

A significant proportion of the book is devoted to the exercises which Jacob and others gave us to facilitate development. The exercises, overall, are quite simple to practise. Jacob made a point of telling us that the exercises may prove helpful in the early stages of development or indeed as aids for regular practice. He told us, that because we are all individuals, it may be that we find some exercises more to our personal temperament and taste than others so we should use those with which we feel a natural affinity. He also pointed out that exercises are only aids. As we develop we are likely to find that awareness flows more spontaneously and we should not create a rigid ritual out of exercises, but flow with the pattern of our own development.

The exercises in this book are not of a hierarchical nature. For Jacob, the key principle seemed to be practise, practise, and then practise again. As time went on, we sometimes felt that people may wish for more 'advanced' exercises. Occasionally Jacob would give us something that was unusual or more demanding in its approach. However, in principle he would often say, that what was needed was more of the same; it was more a case of *deepening and refining* the *quality* of our mediumship through consistent practise, rather than passing through qualitatively different stages or tests.

We have included some of the discussions and feedback that took place during these exercises as they touch upon points and issues of interest. Jacob discusses the main different forms of mental mediumship; clairvoyance, clairaudience and clairsentience, and brings in an invented word of his own 'olfactience,' to indicate the medium of communicating with spirits via smell. This was coined as a joke when it was discovered that one of the members of our development group had a particular skill in this area and would regularly receive scents and smells as a form of communication. From that time Jacob has made regular use of the term, often incorporating some humour.

Jacob's feedback also provides some pointers in attuning to and interpreting messages and symbols. As an example, one person who came to the group complained of being aware of several spirit communicators at once and found this confusing. Jacob advised her to focus in on one of the spirit energies to the exclusion of the others. We have included some of this discussion on 'focussing.' He also frequently stresses the importance of *blending* the images and symbols that we receive in order to become aware of the intended meaning and emphasis of the communicator. This was in response to the tendency of some people attending the group to isolate or compartmentalise their images, instead of connecting them together. Developing this skill calls for a degree of lateral thinking.

Jacob has never underplayed the difficulties involved in spirit communication. However, in spite of the difficulties, he takes the view that the endeavour is worthwhile. He and others have stressed that communication can never be a direct process. Even when it appears most direct, as for instance through trance, it is always one step removed, filtered by the intermediary of our physical senses/processes. Therefore, there is plenty of scope for misunderstandings and erroneous interpretations to creep in. This is particularly so if the medium holds definite views on particular subjects either consciously or unconsciously. It is difficult for spirit communicators to get through the curtain of fixed ideas even when a medium is in deep trance. So difficult can the process of communication be that, at times, providing concrete evidence of survival can seem a forlorn hope. Some members of our group *have* received concrete evidence but the most dramatic evidence has often come incidentally and unexpectedly, rather than when they have been actively seeking it.

Following part three of this book 'Development through Meditation,' we have included the contributions of two Guest Speakers: James and Joseph, and two other members of the Spirit Group, WB, and Carol. Their contributions add a little further insight into certain aspects of the communication process. Perhaps James' contribution is particularly important as he discusses the positive attitude, which we should try to adopt when thinking of relatives and friends who are now in the Spirit World.

We have devoted a short section to trance mediumship and its development. Over the years we've had so many discussions with the

Spirit Group about trance that we could fill a whole book with their communications on this subject. Here we have included just a few of the communications on the key processes and technicalities involved. Also discussed are some of the central principles and issues relating to the development of trance mediumship. Some of these of course are common to all forms of mediumship but trance does bring with it some additional issues.

We debated a bit about the merits of including anything on physical mediumship within the present book. At the time of writing we've been sitting for physical phenomena for six years, but, as we've had only limited success in terms of witnessing phenomena, we would hardly claim to be experts. We have had *some* concrete results such as tugs on people's clothing, taps on parts of the body, spirit voices on our computer and sounds in the room, which we are unable to explain in any other way. We've filmed orbs in infra red light and found our CD player being switched off on a regular basis, without any physical explanation for it.

The sittings for physical phenomena are very enjoyable but it calls for much patience, faith, commitment, and optimism. As with many physical mediumship circles our own has undergone much coming and going of members over the years. This seems to be inevitable when the process of development has such a long time scale. To give the reader the flavour of what we've received on the subject we have included some of the communications from our spirit friends on certain aspects of sitting for physical phenomena. To conclude the book we provide some light-hearted information about the principal members of the Phoenix Group.

We hope that everyone, whether you are in the early stages of development or you are an experienced medium, will find something of interest in this book. Not all of us can be high profile mediums and nor would some wish to be. However, the Spirit Group have told us that, if we *wish* to walk the path of development, most of us *can* develop a degree of awareness. On their part they are ready and waiting for our response with eagerness and love.

Part 1

Mediumship Basics

Chapter 1

Communication with the Spirit World

Hai was asked if he wanted to say anything to begin this book. Below is his reply:

We believe this enterprise is worthwhile because, in spite of the difficulties of communication between the worlds, we may still have communication with each other. Yet it is not without its difficulties and those who engage in this process of communication must acknowledge those difficulties. Those others who would seek to make use of it through mediums or other 'sensitives' must also acknowledge those difficulties and be of patient mind. It is not simple for us to convey information to you, nor is it easy for you to receive it, nor is it easy for *you* to communicate with us. Therefore, there are many difficulties, but in spite of these difficulties our hearts may touch and entwine, and therefore, we believe it is a worthwhile enterprise.

Principles of Communication

On another occasion, Hai told us:

We would say there are general foundations upon which to build. We would say that guided meditation is a valuable foundation to build upon for all development. Beyond this there are different paths for development yet all these paths are intertwined, are interconnected, but we all have our own particular strength in development. This one (referring to the medium) has strength of trance. Others have strength of clairvoyance (seeing,) clairaudience, (hearing) or clairsentience (feeling). Therefore, all have some strength, whether it is of seeing, of hearing, of feeling.

If you wish to develop communication it is a case of experimenting, of trying things out, trying different approaches. It is a matter of relativity this because those who see sometimes also hear or get words and those who get words sometimes see. But we speak of the main strength here and each is advised to find his or her main strength and to build upon that. It might well be that other aspects of development can follow later on as the development is built upon.

When we are attempting spirit communication we must let go of self. We must let go of our critical faculty to enable communication to take place. If we always question what we get we tie ourselves in knots so we must forgo the critical faculty while communication is being allowed. I am not saying that you should get rid of your critical faculty or that you should always suspend your reason, your logic, you understand. But what I do say is that while you are *attempting communication* you need to suspend it and then you must look critically at it later. For if you are questioning all the time, if you are wondering all the time, then this can hinder the ability to communicate because your mind is split.

Hai, also said about communication:

Communication is a wonderful thing for both sides, because as I have said before it is as emotional for people on our side as it is for you on your side and indeed the difficulties are greater from our side because we are more emotional. Our emotions well up in us more, so it is difficult for us.

*   *   *

Hai told us that communication from a spirit guide might take place for many different reasons. Some spirit guides wish to provide evidence of loved ones in the spirit world while others will offer evidence by helping a medium to manifest physical phenomena. Some guides are keen to teach and pass on wisdom but will sometimes provide evidence, often in an incidental way. Below is a very early communication with Hai when, after explaining the above to us, He went on to tell us something of his intentions for future communication through Paul:

> The more you let go the more you open to spirit influence. This is the essence of all communication. This is the main requirement for communication to take place, to be open, empty, and free to allow the influence to express itself. This is no easy task for you or for anybody who wishes to act as a medium for spirit because you have to put yourself in the background so to speak, to allow influence to take place.
>
> We use this opportunity for teaching in the main but we may also be able to help people to have contact with their loved ones. We may also use the opportunity to bring about physical phenomena but our prime concern, our prime aim in making this contact through Paul, is to pass on wisdom and the message of love. We have made it clear that we wish to reach out with this message to those who do not have the opportunity to come to hear us here. (Hai was referring to our first book and our communication through the Internet)

Might you consider a bigger venue to spread the word further?

This is possible but it is for the future and it is a big step for him (the medium) to take. We shall see—we shall see.

Process of Communication

We asked Hai to explain some of the aspects of the process of communication and in the following dialogue he refers particularly to the trance state with the medium, Paul. However, we believe there are common elements that apply to both trance and other forms of mediumship, and therefore, Hai's advice will be applicable to all.

Hai explained:

This process takes place by a blending of our minds. Our minds blend with the medium and it is difficult, because we share each other's thoughts for the time that this goes on. In sharing each other's thoughts there is a transaction that takes place and it is possible that we borrow from the medium's thoughts. However, this does not mean that what we say is invalid. We make use of the medium's mind, thoughts, upbringing, ideas, and beliefs where appropriate. So, it is not like we speak directly to you in the way that you speak directly to each other in daily life; it is more that we speak to you indirectly through the minds of the mediums we use.

This is not to say that we are distant in this communication for we are active participants but it is like; we are on the other side of a foam wall and we press in the foam and create an impression and you will see the impression on the other side but you cannot see our finger prints, you cannot see the fingers with which we make the pattern on the other side of the wall. The foam mediates the impression we make and so it is with the communication, which we are able to do through mediums. It may be more direct over time with development but the refinement is one of relativity.

We must work with the instruments we have but the message, the essence of what we try to convey usually succeeds in coming through. We stir the stick in the pool and create ripples and you see the ripples. The ripples are an accurate reflection of the consequences of the stick being stirred in the water but unless you were in the place where the stick was being stirred all you would see on the far side of the lake would be the ripples which it creates and this may be another useful analogy for you.

One circle member decided to change tack and asked:

Hai, could a group of people who were working in the way we do, give a message through their spirit group to be passed on to another group of people working in the same way?

It may be possible but it is fraught with difficulties because of various levels of communication and different connections that will have to take place, but in principle it is possible.

She continued with her question:
Is it easier to contact a spirit when they have only just passed over than if they have been there a long time? Are they more receptive to our responses when they first pass over?

When they first pass over they are nearer to your vibrational rate, are nearer your plane; this is generally so. Therefore, their vibration at this time is of a heaviness, which can associate more easily with your plane. This makes communication easier, more fluent sometimes than would be the case for someone on a plane more removed from your earthly vibrational rate. Time does not matter in terms of this. It is more to do with the vibrational rate and the plane in which we live.

So does that mean that it is easier to communicate with spirits on the astral plane?

Well, the astral plane is nearer your vibrational rate; therefore, it's easier from that point of view to communicate with spirits in that plane. But you must be careful in communicating with spirits in the astral plane, Janice, for they are a right mixed bunch. (Laughter)

I understand that we have to raise our vibration to meet spirit. How do we know when we are doing that?

Hai was still in his humorous mode and replied:

Well you are all doing a pretty good job now for you are all taking to me.

* * *

One night WB (spirit scientist) answered questions on the Process of Communication and Linking

How does it work then, WB, when a medium just senses something without really knowing where it has come from?

There are times when the blending is so smooth that you may not be aware of our presence but the thought may well have been planted by us. In some ways this blending is very smooth, very effective. However, simply because it is so smooth and effective people may not always be aware of the fact that it comes from an outside source, because outside and inside are blended in one, melded together smoothly, so there is not the same sense of something coming from outside. This can be effective of course but it provides problems to the person because they do not have this sense of someone coming to them from outside.

This is the dilemma and the difficulty for you because you believe it might be your imagination or creativity and sometimes it may indeed be that. However, it may also be because we have influenced you and the influencing has been so smooth, so effective, that you are not aware of it coming from outside. You must leave yourselves open to all possibilities. The mind can close you down. You must be open.

Does a medium's own vibration or frequency, limit them to who they can talk to in spirit, or does it broaden out when they become more experienced?

It is most important to reach out, simply to reach out, and to focus. As you progress and develop ability to sense spirits the ability to refine that attunement to particular spirits develops as you practise. Therefore, when you sense a particular spirit you are able to attune to them more readily, more quickly, in a more refined way. It is a focusing in. It is like the radio, you have to press one button to get you where you want and the other to fine tune the frequency. It is like that when attuning to spirits. When you first start the adjustment it is rather coarse. It is rather rough and ready perhaps, and so you may find that when you attune to spirit there are other spirits on the periphery. The wavelengths are a bit jumbled perhaps at times, but as you progress and become more practised you are able to turn the fine tune up and focus much more specifically, narrowly, on the spirit you wish to focus upon. It is practise and patience and discipline. Some never learn to fine tune because they do not practise in the right way. They do not make a point of fine tuning; trying to fine tune; it comes with practise.

If a medium wants to give a message to a particular person, is it possible for the medium to attract a spirit that the person would have known?

Each person here has links with those in spirit, and therefore, you pick up on one of those links and connect with the spirit concerned, but of course some links are more active than others at different times. It is like in your own lives. You have many associates, many friends, many people you know, but not all of those links are active at one time. It would be impossible would it not, to conduct your lives if it was otherwise. Therefore, links with your spirit friends also vary in the degree of activity during the day and over time, but you may pick up on those links and fine tune into them.

Imagery/Symbolism/Interpreting

Hai began the question and answer session below by saying:

The deepest reality, the deepest truth, is often best conveyed through imagery rather than words because of the limitations of words which we have discussed before. Images can overcome the contradictions and the duality of words sometimes. It is also easier, with the exception of the present mode, which I am using, (trance mediumship) for us to place an image in your minds than it is to create a clear message using words. However, in general terms, when we try and convey messages to mediums, there is a power in an image that would take many words to convey the same meaning.

So the skill of the medium is the interpretation of the image?

Yes. Sometimes we are able to convey the appropriate way to interpret the image. We can convey the *feeling* with the image, about the direction in which it should be interpreted and this is safer than an image alone. As you know, images as with words can be interpreted in different ways. We often convey an impression and sense of how the medium should work with the image. Our communication also has this strong imagery that we use to communicate our thoughts. Our communications use imagery quite a lot and we also convey emotions more directly than you are able to, so we convey these things when we work with mediums.

So as well as the mind's thoughts, is it also the picture, which is given for communication?

Yes we can convey an image within the message.

Is there any limit to the distance which you can transmit these thoughts and images if you want to contact somebody?

We have only to think of the person and we may then convey a message to them. Distance is only relative and is not meaningful here or in the spirit worlds but in the spirit worlds this reality is more evident.

Do the same images mean the same thing each time or does it vary?

The meanings of the symbols can vary depending upon the spirit who gives them and upon the person who receives them. There has to be a melding, synchronicity in the way they understand the meanings for the message to be accurately received. This is not always easy.

Couldn't this be confusing to the medium?

It could be, yet it is possible to receive accurate images this way in spite of the difficulties.

How important is it that we work on our visualisation?

It is important. It is important because the more you practise, as with any art or skill, the more you will develop, so it is important. You should retain your critical faculty though which you have spoken of amongst yourselves tonight. You should test the visions, the images that you are receiving.

Foretelling the Future:

Why don't prophetic messages always come true, Hai?

First communication is difficult. It is not easy. Even with the present medium it is not easy, because the medium's mind can influence things. This is the case with others, who receive messages in visual form or through hearing or sensing. They have to interpret what they are given and error can creep in. There can also be difficulties if messages pertain to the future because the future is not written in stone. We can sometimes detect the flow, we can attempt to predict based upon the flow or the pattern, but it is like a flow in that it is not fixed in an absolute sense, and therefore, the future can vary from the pattern that we see and which we try to use to predict the future. In the final analysis you all have free will and this can change the course of events so we should be wary of those who say with absolute certainty that they can tell us our future.

*   *   *

On another occasion Hai was again asked about predicting the future but this time the question had a different slant to it. After answering the original question, Hai then went on to advise what a medium could do when having an 'off' day.

*I was wondering if we can view your world in a certain way, could you view **another** world in the same way?*

We can attune to the past when we come to your earthly plane, to the vibration of the past, which is contained within the vibration of the present.

So this theory that time applies to everything is not always relevant then depending on where you are?

Time is all encompassed by the reality within the One Mind and to that extent it is malleable, it is not linear, it is not fixed. It is not determined.

Can you also connect with the future?

We can connect with the future based upon the vibration of the present, which carries within its own ebb and flow the imprint, the image, of the future.

Can you see a long way ahead?
We can see a long way ahead but the more ahead you look, the further in the distance, into the future you look, the more risk there is of going astray with your interpretation.

So in our terms how far can you see ahead?
There are possibilities as we look into the future but these possibilities are not fixed as we have said before; they are not fixed. Therefore, we cannot say with one-hundred-percent certainty what will transpire but we will be fairly sure of what will transpire.

I was just wondering how fixed say, one year ahead would be?
Hai smiled:
We can see you all enjoying yourselves a year from now. Time is not solid. Time is malleable. Time is changeable. The pattern of what will transpire through the passing of time is malleable, is fluid.

When a medium gives a predictive message, is it something they perceive or have they been given the information by spirit. I've found that some predictions have sometimes taken two years to transpire?
They are unwise often to be too precise in their message of time, for you know we have often talked of difficulties of communication. Even if we think we get our message across from our side their mind must interpret our message. Therefore, there are many points where the message may go wrong. The more precise the point that we wish to convey, the more precise the message which the medium may give, the more points of difficulty there are, the greater the likelihood of things going astray. Therefore, it is difficult this preciseness, because over time it is hard to achieve with great accuracy and certainty. It is not that we cannot sometimes achieve it but mediums would be well to not be too overconfident in stating exact times.

Sometimes though it is obvious that a medium is not having a good day. Would it be better if they just said they couldn't get anything that day and finish rather than struggling on?
Well it would be best to do this you are quite right because sometimes it is as if we have two beacons, two torches, or flames standing in space. And we need these two torches to be seen by both sides for communication to take place. Sometimes there is a fog in the middle distance between these torches and we may only see a flicker of a flame, far from seeing the full torch. Therefore, these conditions are not ideal, they are not satisfactory for communication, and when these

conditions prevail it would be better to call it a day and say; "Well things are not working today, we will try tomorrow."

It is best to do this but there are times you know, when your mediums go on the platform, and they feel it is like a plank walking out from a ship. And rather than thinking; "well if this does not work I will just turn around and walk the plank back onto the ship," they feel that they have no choice and that they either must perform or they must jump into the devouring ocean. But this is not a sensible way to view this thing for it's all experimentation. Even the best of mediums may find they are not good sometimes and so communication is hindered to a greater or lesser extent. Therefore, it is far better, as you say, David, not to proceed but to cut our losses for the day and return on the morrow.

What makes the best of mediums rather than one who has difficulties then, Hai?

Every medium may have difficulties. There are some who have more strength than others but may still have difficulties on certain days, and therefore, it may transpire that they too should say; "I am sorry my friends, this is not a good day for me. It would be best to come back another day."

Some mediums are so certain and confident. They don't seem to get anything wrong. Is it a particular attunement?

Well this can be dangerous also for confidence is not always accuracy and there are those who are confident but not accurate. There are those who are not confident but who are accurate. And there is every variation in between. It is like everything else though, that if there is practise the more likelihood there is of success, of overcoming difficulties. But if someone has turned the tap off for the day it is better to walk away rather than try to turn it with a wrench.

Going back to my last question, if a medium is having difficulty could he/she switch to Psychometry (holding a small item to link with someone in spirit) or would they be prevented from that also?

They may get something that way but it is for them to judge whether they should proceed. They would need to consider whether they have enough connection, enough energy, enough awareness, and enough attunement to have some degree of success or not. There may be other times where it is better to draw a line under any attempt to connect with spirit or with messages, for conditions are not right. It is always possible to turn the event into something enjoyable even though people may be disappointed as to the original purpose of the meeting. The event can be turned into something enjoyable if people are resourceful, if they are loving and giving enough, patient and tolerant enough with each other.

So in those circumstances you would have to be creative would you not?

You would have to be creative yes, but if those who are on the platform together were to help each other to be creative, there is no reason why a successful event could not take place. We after all, are in a world where we must love each other. If there is good will, if there is harmony, if there is love and respect for each other, we can turn any event into a successful and enjoyable event.

*   *   *

One night our spirit scientist, WB, was asked a question along a similar theme:

WB, my family who have passed often tell me things in my dreams that later come true.

Yes, as we have said before we can see the pattern, can see the flow in the river, and in some small measure we may sometimes be able to say this will come to pass or that will come to pass. But we are not keen to divulge this on a regular basis for we feel there are inherent dangers here because you as human beings may believe that the pattern is written for you, that it cannot be changed, that it will not change. But you can affect the flow; affect the direction your life will take. You can affect the flow of the waters through your choices, free will. For if this was not the case what would be the point of you being here. If all were determined from the moment of birth, there would be no point whatsoever.

Opening up/Closing down

One of our circle members was developing trance mediumship and Eileen found herself discussing his development with Davia, our spirit gatekeeper/manager. She explained that John had felt the energy come through at an inconvenient time and asked Davia for his comments.

Those of you who've read our first book will already be familiar with Davia's particular brand of humour especially when he decides to take on the role of raising the energies. Davia does have a more serious side, which he only shows on rare occasions; this was not one of them.

In the following communication, Davia, as usual, could not resist the odd joke here and there and we've printed the communication unedited in an attempt to demonstrate some of the spirit humour that we've come to love so much. In spite of the reader having to extract the serious content from Davia's humour we feel that there is something of particular interest here about opening up to spirit and closing down again afterwards. Eileen began by commenting:

It was difficult for John when the spirit started to come through in that way. I thought spirit would only come through when it was convenient.

Davia laughed raucously and replied:
Convenient to **us**, yes. *You* create a link so you must not think of spirit if it is not convenient for you, because (laughing again) it may be convenient for us but inconvenient for him.

When we'd all finished laughing Eileen persisted with another question.

But, Davia, can you not see where the person is when the link is made?
I can see all manner of things, Eileen but if he reaches out he creates a link. You've got to take some control, some responsibility for the time you link.
So is it like a pipe with the water running through it, if it's not turned off?
Davia replied:
Or if you turn the tap on it will flow, so you need to turn the tap off, and only when you want to link should you turn it on.
Do people automatically close down after sitting in meditation?
Well you say automatically but it is more to do with the fact that you shift your mind, and in shifting your mind to something else or some other thoughts *you* switch off, ground yourself, disconnect. It is not automatic as you suggest. It is if you change your focus; change your focus of your mind, then that disconnects from our energies.
Some leaders of development groups suggest that you need to close each chakra individually each time after meditation or communication with spirit.

Davia, still in top form, replied:

> Well you can do that you know, you can close all your chakras, yes, but I know another way as well which is very good for closing down. Well you go outside and you jump in your pond. I can guarantee that this will disconnect you and ground you very effectively.

When we'd all finished laughing Eileen asked:

> *If Paul and I talk together about spirit, are we automatically opening ourselves up?*
>
> Sometimes it can create a pattern in your mind which then connects with us or other spirits so you'd better watch for that but this is not to say you must not talk. You must be aware that sometimes it can create a pattern in your mind which means you connect because you send out a beam if you like.

*   *   *

On another occasion WB was asked a question on the same theme:

> *If you picked up a spirit vibration and it was not convenient at that particular time to communicate with them, how would you pass this information to them?*
>
> Simply tell them that it is not an appropriate time for the communication to take place. You simply state this to them and **move your mind on mentally** as well. This is the key, move your mind on, do something else to do with the physical world in your daily life, and in moving your mind on you break the link, you withdraw it for the moment. It is important to develop this discipline.

Impact of Mediumship on the Medium

One of our circle members asked about a book he'd been reading. The book was written by a medium that believed that she had become ill from working with spirit. He asked Hai:

Is it possible to become ill from working too hard with spirit?

You must use your judgement as in all other things. You must use moderation. This was a golden saying of the Buddha; "moderation in all things." It is true we must use moderation in everything we do. Excess is not to be desired in anything. It spoils what we can do. It exhausts when it should not exhaust us so she should use her judgement and use moderation.

Why don't the spirits who work with her tell her to have a rest?

Well we have spoken to you of this before. When you reach out to us you act as a magnet and you draw us to you. It is not **we** imposing on you. You act as a willing channel. You attract us like a magnet and you use us as much as we use you. You must use your own responsibility, your own judgement to decide what is appropriate, what is reasonable and desirable.

So you need a point of balance then.

Just so, balance. People must use their judgement, they must take responsibility; this is a golden rule. We are responsible for our own actions. We are responsible for our own lives and how we use them. We must stay the captain of our ship.

On another night Hai was asked:

Some mediums seem very tired after giving sittings; can you tell me why this happens, Hai?

It partly depends upon the smoothness of the blend and the ease of the link. If the link is smooth, easy, and harmonious, then there should not be too much of a feeling of tiredness; so this will be variable. In the early stages a harmonious link is not always easy to achieve and it is like I have said before, it is almost like a car shifting into gear. If the shift is smooth there is no shudder in the car's movement along the road, but if the gear does not shift smoothly then the car shudders. It is similar with the medium. If there is a slight shuddering this can create tiredness, so it is an art; it is an art from our side also.

Another member of the group commented:

I felt very drained when I came away from the meditation at the church development circle last night. Was it to do with the particular energies within the group?

There are very many variables. If you have groups with changing members then obviously people take time to get used to each other and this in itself can cause a draining experience. It is not so much to do with the blending of the energy, unless the blending of the energy is inharmonious because the people are inharmonious.

Is there anything we can do to protect ourselves from this draining?

It is not a matter of protection; it is a matter of the development of the skill, of attunement. It is not too detrimental in any event; it is merely a slight tiring, which can be recuperated. There is nothing in itself that is draining in communication with spirit, but you know yourselves that if you exert your physical bodies, if you have to concentrate for any length of time, then you will feel natural tiredness. This is only to be expected and can arise from communication because you are using your usual faculties along with the faculties of linking with spirit. However, there is a reinvigorating aspect to the energy that you receive by working with spirit, so there is a trade off you might say.

If you ask for the protection of the white light would that help?

The white light is symbolic, David. It is not so much a reality of itself, it is you, asking for simple help, simple protection and assistance, and we respond to that.

So in a way it does exist then, the white light?

Symbolically: in the sense of which you speak.

Does the person receiving the communication via the medium cause the draining effect on the medium?

Generally not but again I say to you that if you had a discussion with a person who was traumatised, who was anxious, who was troubled in mind, you would feel drained, would you not, at the end of that discussion? So the same applies if you were working with such a person and communicating with spirit simultaneously.

So is there nothing that could be done to prevent that?

There is an art, as they say, and with a development of the art the art grows skilful and there is less likelihood of the draining affect.

However, you always have the usual physical conditions of life that you have to contend with.

I was wondering, if people don't stop for a break and don't eat etc, would that make them physically tired?

As always it is best to have moderation in all things and to be sensible with the discipline of communication.

I heard of one medium that appeared to keep herself deliberately hungry because she thought it helped her to communicate more clearly with spirit.

This amused Hai and he replied:

She may communicate more clearly with her hallucinations if she kept that up!

Maintaining equilibrium

Hai's advice was sought on how to find peace and equilibrium. He told us:

You should go within yourself and you should create for yourself an inner sanctuary, an inner sanctuary of great peace, of great beauty, of great gentleness and support. You should imagine this inner sanctuary in which you feel totally safe, totally free, totally at peace and you should spend some little time in this sanctuary each day. Gradually you may find that your visits to your special sanctuary may ease your mind and bring back your equilibrium. Equilibrium is a very important thing for you in your lives, a very important thing. For your world does not encourage it, your world does not facilitate it, but it is very important for without it you loose your balance, you loose your perspective on your life.

Is this a form of meditation?

It is a form of meditation. It is like you do with Isleen (member of the Spirit Group) on her guided meditations but rather than following her journey, *you* create the journey and the special place yourself. It may be a room; it may be a scene by a lakeside, or in the middle of the mountains; it does not matter. It is where you feel comfortable, where you feel at your ease, where you feel safe; this is what is important. You should become familiar with this place and this is where it differs from Isleen's meditations. You should create a special place where you feel at home and feel familiar with. You should furnish it with objects that you find comforting and which will put you at your ease, so when you return to this special place it is so familiar to you that it becomes easier and easier each time you visit it.

Early advice for the development of mediumship

Below is a conversation that took place between Hai and our Home Circle in the early days when we were discussing the possibility of broadening out our communication. We decided to print the conversation here because in this communication Hai answers many questions that we feel will be of interest to those who are just beginning with their development.

A circle member asked:

You said we could use some of our time for development. What form would that take?
We could do further experiments like we did the other night. We could try to develop clairvoyance. We could try to develop trance for those of you who wished it but the trance must be separate to other situations.
Do these stages of development provide grounding for our development?
Well, developments do not happen overnight but there can be a gradual process of development, with certain spurts forward. It may seem like it is happening overnight but there has been much groundwork done to bring this about. So we build a foundation and we build on the foundation, and as we build it is easier to start to reach the heights like a pyramid. The base of the pyramid is large, yes, large and square, but as we build it up it becomes higher and higher and it becomes easier to reach higher and higher. For as we build each layer the materials are less as we reach the heights.
People who are multitalented i.e. they are healers, clairvoyants, and trance mediums, do they need to start another pyramid or can they use the same one?

Hai replied with amusement:

You are building tombs of multi generations of pharaohs now. Ah but we do not need all these magnificent pyramids, no. Let us take your analogy of multi pyramids further. Let us say that we build up our pyramid from the foundation, from the base and we start to build this foundation and we start to put a lot of effort, a lot of time and material into this base. It is much hard work, so we build this massive base, and we carry on building our pyramid. So it gets higher and higher and then we think to ourselves; "Ah we shall not build a pyramid after all, we will build a mountain instead." So instead of having one pinnacle, one point, we decide to build a number of pinnacles, just like a mountain and we decide we shall have one pinnacle which is higher than the rest and we will have a couple of other pinnacles which will be of similar height and we will have a couple of other pinnacles to be lower in height compared to the higher ones.

So we may compare this with the development, with the abilities of which you speak. Say for arguments sake a medium is most gifted, is developed most, in the trance ability, and so we would compare this pinnacle of this new mountain we have built to the highest one, the highest pinnacle. But say this trance medium also has some ability in clairvoyance and healing and let us say for arguments sake the ability in these two areas is equal, so we can compare these abilities with the two lower pinnacles not as high as the highest but still quite high. Then we come to the two final ones and there is perhaps lesser ability in these areas so we can say that perhaps the person is less able in the psychic area and is less able in the clairsentience area. There is some ability, but these peaks are lesser than the other three. Therefore, on the one foundation all the five skills have potential for development but perhaps there may only be two or three which can be strongly developed.

If we do begin these development nights, would they start with a meditation?

The meditation does indeed prepare the ground for some of these abilities. It provides practise and experiences that are conducive and helpful to development. But we may build on this to consider other ways forward, other ways of developing.

How we sense spirits

Hai was asked:

Is it correct that the temperature around us changes when spirit beings are present?
You will find that this will vary depending upon both the spirit energy and your energy for it is the *transaction* between the energies of yourself and the spirit being, which you experience. Therefore, some may experience certain spirits as cold, some may experience the same spirit as warm. A *transaction* of energies is important here not that all spirits are cold or all spirits are warm.
What do you mean by transaction?
The transaction of energies between your energies and those of the spirit being who manifests for you, who wish to contact you to make their presence known.

Eileen commented that Paul had experienced a particular spirit, who had come through the previous week, as a very cold energy. Hai answered:

Ah, earth, cold, strong energy.

This prompted another question:

So what is stronger energy, Hai, cold or hot?
Strong energy is strong energy whether cold or hot.
What is the easiest way for a spirit to let us know of his presence?

Hai answered with humour:

It would be easiest to poke you in the back but many find this quite difficult to achieve. Seriously though, it would be easiest to impact upon your mind, to place a thought there, to place awareness of themselves in your mind through some image, through some symbol. This is the easiest way for many spirits to make their presence known.
If you speak of physical phenomena, affecting the physical world, then this is a different matter. We may find it easier to impress an image on your photographic film. This may be easier than other forms of manifestation. But we may also move objects or create noises. We

may also manifest images of ourselves, which seem to be solid but are not necessarily solid.

The questioner commented that she had tried impressing images of spirit on film but it had not worked. She asked Hai if this meant that the spirit did not want to be photographed. He replied:

> No, it may be that they do not have the technical know how. It may be that the energies are not quite right and the opportunities are not quite in place, that they need help in order to manifest, as they would wish. So there are many reasons why we may not achieve this thing.
> *Is it harder for you to manifest, or move something?*
> It depends upon the energies available to us but it is generally more difficult to manifest by making physical movement than it is by impressing images onto photographic plates or similar objects.
>
> *Hai, do you use more energy than other spirits because you come from a different plane?*
> Yes we do use more energy. We use more energy than those who are nearer to your own plane.
> *How do you sustain that energy?*
> We may draw upon the pool of energy, the pool of energy that not only you contribute but also spirits on our side contribute.

Contact with loved ones in the Spirit World

Hai was asked:

> *If we have a loved one in the spirit world, is it unreasonable to call on that loved one if we are distressed?*
> You are connected to your loved ones by an invisible link, if you wish to think of it in this way, for if you send your thoughts out to them they assuredly will sense those thoughts and will be drawn to you. But we would encourage you to think of the impact of your thoughts on your loved ones in spirit. You should think of them in a similar way to how you would have thought of them on the earth plane. They are sensitive to your needs, they are responsive to your needs, and they are concerned for your needs. However, you know

yourself if you had a child, a daughter or son, who was constantly pestering you for help for their worries over this and that, and so forth, then this would become wearing would it not, after a while.

So we should think on this and we should think on this principle when we are reaching out to our loved ones. They assuredly want us to reach out to them. They assuredly are concerned about us, about our needs and will lovingly come to us when our need is great, but we should play the role of the sensitive child who does not pester or worry the parent overly. You follow me? As we have said before, emotions on our side are rather more intense than for you and so this is something you should consider.

Is that because of heightened sensitivity?

It is because of the higher vibration on which we operate and though the human body may magnify certain sensations it may dampen other sensations. Without the human body our emotions may be more pronounced sometimes. Emotion is energy, is it not, and therefore, emotional energy with less constraint may become more heightened. This is one reason why we should try and bring our emotions under control while we are on the earth plane rather than leaving this task to the spirit lands where the task may be more difficult to achieve.

So by doing that we could help ourselves in the spirit world?

You help yourself in every world.

Another member of the group asked:

Do our loved ones in spirit connect with us all the time, or do they come during special events?

They have awareness of you all the time, but it is like a thought in the background, awareness of the bond and the connection. This is not intrusive upon their existence yet there is an awareness, and when they wish, they can connect with you more fully. It is like—how shall I say; It is like, if you require spectacles and your optician puts a pair of spectacles in front of your eyes, but they are out of focus and he needs to adjust, manipulate, the focus. Sometimes the words in front of you will become crystal clear. At other times they will be blurred. So it is a bit like this; your loved ones may bring you into clear focus, as clear as the print upon the paper, and at other times you may be a bit more of a blur in the background.

So, if there is something that they want to participate in they can quickly bring us into focus can they?

Yes, or if they wish merely to attune to you at a certain moment, at a certain time.

So they don't ever miss anything, even if it's unplanned?

Hai smiled and replied:

You should not worry about them missing anything; rather you should take comfort from the possibility that they might not know everything.

How Spirits present themselves to the Medium

Hai was asked:

Would a medium sometimes see a younger version of the person passed over?

This may be so but is not necessarily so for the spirit may manifest according to need, according to the situation and context, according to peoples expectations. Therefore, our manifestation may vary, even from time to time, as we choose a particular manifestation to link with those who come to meet us. We may manifest as a young child on one occasion and as an adult on another. We use these manifestations in a skilful way according to the needs of the moment, according to the needs of those who are there.

Chapter 2

Influence of Guides and Helpers

In this chapter Hai covers questions on Guides and Helpers. He offers advice on how we can connect with our guides and explains how they may attempt to influence us.

Hai begins by answering a question from one regular group member who asks whether some of our thoughts are planted in our minds by spirit. Further questions lead on from this with the person becoming quite persistent and wanting to receive concrete answers to her questions. This caused Hai to go into what Eileen often describes as his 'tease' mode. Hai is never unkind and his teasing usually has the effect of raising the energies in the group.

How we are inspired by Spirit

Hai was asked:

When we suddenly get an idea in our head and have been looking for an answer, is that spirit intervention or just coincidence?
Well this may be that you are embarking on a life course which is meant to be. It is not always necessary to have spirit intervention as such, but it may be that the currents of the universe push you in a particular direction; the currents that you chose to ride when you came on the earth plane this time. Therefore, the currents push you in this direction for it is part of your life purpose being here.

If we get words which could be appropriate to our circumstances is that help from the spirit world?
We may inspire you. We may push words in your mind to help you, to give you something to reflect upon, to help you to decide what

you will do. So it is possible. The two worlds are not separate. The two worlds are not diverse; they are intermingling with each other all the time. Therefore, we might quite often instil, put words in your mouth, to help you reflect upon. However, you must remember that it is a two-way flow and your thoughts will find their way to us and have an impact upon us. So there is no difference here, there is no division here, the worlds interpenetrate, and minds interpenetrate, at a fundamental level.

So if I was thinking something, you could pick that up?

Yes, because your wavelength might resonate with my wavelength and I may, therefore, pick up your thought, your impulse. But this is more likely to happen when we have forged a connection with certain people on the earth plane.

Sometimes I am not always sure that my 'gut feeling' is right or wrong but then I look for a sign to seek confirmation. So if I get that confirmation should I go with the flow?

You cannot find this answer you seek, cannot find this *definite* answer, for it does not work like that. For you may have an impulse and then you may have a thought; you may then have another thought, so you think; "ah is this my friends in the spirit world to inspire me, to push me to go in this direction." But the reality is; you must make your own choice, your own decision based upon your best assessment of what you must do, of what is involved with the decision that you must make.

So if something is just meant to be will it just flow without any problems?

Hai was in his tease mode. He smiled and said:

Meant to be? You have to make your own decisions; **you** have to make your own decisions. I know some things that flow exceedingly well may cause mayhem for people, yes, so it is not about going smoothly, exceedingly well. It may be that some things do go extraordinarily well for you and it is because things have come together. The current has come together for you to buoy you along on the river towards a particular direction, a particular spot. But you must trust, you must go with your trust. If you wish for the best, the best for you and the best for others, then you will be buoyed upon the current and you will be safe in the current. You may not be comfortable (smiling) but you will be safe. You will grow in those directions that you need to grow. You will be carried along the river in the way you need to be carried along the river. But if you try to make some mathematical formula out of this it will not do, it will not work. Then it becomes like; I throw a dice, I throw a six, everything is all right. Yes? But you must *know* that even if you throw and it is not a six, it is still all right.

Contacting Guides

Hai gave the following advice when a visitor to the group asked how she could contact her guide. He told her:

You should reach out to your spirit guide. You should reach out with your heart and mind and you should eventually sense them in some way or other. You may sense their energy, you may sense an image, and you may feel their presence. You may have thoughts and images planted in your mind unexpectedly. All these ways may be indications that you have made contact so you should proceed in this way. Once the contact is established the link can grow stronger. You should practise every day or as regularly as you can. It is a matter of consistency, a matter of regular persistent practise.

I notice you referred to guides. You told us once that you preferred another expression.

I do not prefer any expression in truth, for we are all seekers on the path, we are all friends together on the path. The fact that *we* have rounded the next bend, the fact that *we* stand a little further up the hill is no cause to place us on a pedestal, is no reason to rely on us for the forward path. We may assist, we may help you to develop, but you must have responsibility for your own lives. You are mature beings in your own right and you have responsibility and the right to make your own decisions.

Would a guide work exclusively with one person on the earth plane or would he help many different people at the same time?

There is no need that this person (guide) be restricted to one. They may help others also but in saying this there is no diminishment of the help that can be offered, for we are not bound by your limitations.

By helping us, does this in some way help the guide to move on? Do they learn from us?

We do not necessarily learn *from* you but we learn from giving our love *to* you. We learn through giving our assistance to you and we learn from giving our compassion to you. But this is the nature of it. It is not that we necessarily learn directly from you, but nevertheless, we learn through adopting our role, through the act of giving assistance to you, and in this you give us your gift for you give us the gift of the opportunity of offering assistance and love.

On another occasion Hai was asked:

Are guides capable of performing things like switching lights and radios on to prove they are around?

Not generally but it can happen on occasion. We have here (in our house) an instance of a computer being talked through (by a spirit entity) so it is possible. But we would not encourage you to put us to too many tests. The most important thing is to establish the relationship. So you reach out to us, you create a space in which we may contact you, then you will come to recognise and to know us and you will come to know the relationship. You will then begin to establish a close relationship with your guides.

So we suggest you create this space through meditation, through meditative practices, through attuning yourself to us as we to you, for it is a two way process. It is a partnership. Therefore, we suggest you open yourself and still your mind. You will then enable contact by your guides and together you work, together. (Smiling) If you set too many tasks you are liable to attract the wrong type. Some spirits are more close to the earthly vibration, they dabble in things and are more able to switch lights on and off. If you put a test to your guide to switch a light on and off; you may get the light switched on and off but perhaps by some unsavoury type. You follow me? This is nothing to worry about. They are just mischief-makers but why allow them room for their mischief.

Do the mischief-makers tend to linger or do they go away of their own accord?

They go away if they get bored. Like on earth, if you have a nuisance person and you pay them attention they become a bigger nuisance. They come back because they get a reaction from you. They like the reaction so they come back again. It is the same with a mischievous spirit. You react, they get the reaction, and they come back for more and say; "Ah, this is a good time for me; this person gives me a good show when I intervene." (Jacob also comments on this in a later chapter)

Guides always seem to be high up spirits. We never seem to hear of; for example, a guide who worked down a mine or was from an ordinary working class background.

Hai modestly replied:
Well I'm not 'high up' as you say, Janice. (We don't think the rest of the Spirit Group would agree)

Hai went on to say:
Yes I can understand what you are trying to say but the reasons for this may be varied. This is one reason: Your Tom who lived down the road, may have been an Egyptian priest in a past life but if he had the choice of representing himself, coming back, as Tom down the road or an Egyptian prince or priest, what do you think he would choose?

Janice replied laughing:
Tom, down the road.
Hai smiled and responded:
You make a joke. They come as seems more fitting for the role. So this is one reason. However, another reason perhaps is that the person (medium) may distort the connection, or they have a preoccupation with the kind of guide they want. Sometimes they think to themselves, not always consciously but deep inside the mind, that perhaps they don't want any old shoddy guide, any old stupid guide, or any old commonplace guide. They want the guide with the right face, the right status, so they would interpret and distort the energy of this guide to their own need. Therefore, to be accepted by the person, the guides may represent themselves in a particular way; this is not important to us. What is important is the connection and the message which we convey. It is not important whether we are who we say we are. I realise that you may find this funny or strange.

Janice had been on the receiving end of Hai's teasing in the past and was in a playful mood. She asked:

*So are **you**, Hai?*

Well it so happens I am on this occasion. But you follow me; the message to us is all-important, not the identity of the guide, though there are those who get hung up with the identity of the guide.

Is it an ego thing then, with some mediums, that they have a guide who was considered an evolved being when on the earth plane?

Yes, this may be so but it is the message of love that is important. This is a minor problem of ego, people wanting, preferring a particular kind of guide. It is a minor problem of ego.

A minor problem, I thought ego was a major problem, Hai.

Yes you are right, ego is a major problem, but in the scheme of things having a hang up about a private guide is a small-scale problem of ego compared to big scale problems of ego. But this, as with all else, they must put down in time and be open to the truth from whatever source it comes.

*   *   *

One night before our usual meditation Isleen was asked about guides:

Hai has said that the bond of love is always there and can never be broken, how do I make the bond between my guide and myself stronger, Isleen?

You reach out to him. If you reach out to any of us we will meet you halfway. You have only to reach out to us with feelings of love as we reach to you with feelings of love, and we meet together in love. The vibration we each set up gives us both an infallible homing signal.

So you must reach out to your guide in this way. Imagine his image, imagine him standing before you. Reach out to him with your feelings and your thoughts and he will reach out to you also and you will draw closer to each other. But you should not be worried if you do not sense us all the time in a definite way, because even though you do not sense us we are with you, we are not far away. Your ability to sense us will fluctuate. This does not mean that we are any further away from you. You must press on calmly, quietly, in confidence and trust.

*   *   *

We find that as people come regularly to our group they form a deep affection and affinity to the Spirit Group members and in particular with Hai. One of our regular members had been at another venue where Hai had communicated. He asked Hai about the reaction he'd felt.

Last week when you spoke through Paul at another venue, I felt your voice drawing me, is it the link we have formed here which caused that?
We've formed an affinity with you who sit regularly, so our energies are linked in this affinity. Therefore, when I speak you may feel a pull; you may feel this pull because of the energy link between us. It is like your brotherhood of which you spoke downstairs earlier. (Hai was referring to a conversation we'd had earlier about the White Eagle Brotherhood)

Guides & Mediumship

When our circle meets each member usually brings along at least one question. Often this one question will lead to others and the conversation flows easily. However, one night we had two new visitors to the circle. They were understandably hesitant about being the first to speak but even the regular members of the group seemed at a loss for a question to ask. There was a brief silence. Davia (spirit gatekeeper) was obviously in the background commenting to Hai on the silence when eventually Hai laughed and said:

Davia says he is ready to pack up and go home if you do not produce the goods.

This brought about much laughter, which had the effect of lightening the situation. The questions started to flow.

Hai was asked:
Do you have one guide that stays with you throughout life, or do they change?
Hai shakes his head and says:
There are many people, who help you, Carol, yes, many people who may help you. But it is often the case that one particular guide

will stay with you for some time. Sometimes your guide may stay with you for your life, but at other times it may be that there is a need for the guide to be changed, to move on because your needs change. Your needs are of paramount importance to us; therefore, it is this which we allocate the guide for, not the needs of the guide. If your needs change, we can change the guide to meet your needs. It is like a relay race sometimes. The guide can take you on so far but then must hand on the batten to the next guide who can take you further. You follow me? (Smiles) So you may think that *you* get tired but think about the poor guides running the relay race.

Would a new guide communicate with us in a different way?

Yes it may be that they will connect with you in a different way and by this you will know that there has been a change or there is a change occurring. If they did not communicate with you in a slightly different way you would be oblivious to the change though you may sense the change in energy. But it may be that sometimes you have got used to a guide approaching you from a particular direction, say the left of your body and you become aware of an entrance, a connection behind perhaps, indicating a new energy source, new guide. This is one way that we may convey the change that is occurring. But you may be sensitive to the changing energy at a more subtle level depending upon how developed you are, how attuned you are, to your guide.

Does the guide actually come into our aura?

Yes, they come into the aura and this is how you will know and sense them but they do not connect directly; they do not come into *you* as such.

Family & Friends as helpers

Hai was asked:

Are guides spirits that we knew when on the earth plane, like relatives or friends?

Not generally so. It may be that your relatives or friends are helpers for you and even work with your guides to help you but generally a guide is someone who is not closely related to you. It is possible on occasion that it may be someone deep from your ancestral past but it is rare for it to be someone who is close to you in your family linkage. It is more often someone else who is not known to your family linkage. This is the usual state of affairs.

Clairvoyants tend to say that it's either a close relative or a loved one who is caring for you from the spirit world.

No these are helpers, they are helping you, and they are guardians, if you wish to view it this way, but they are not often spiritually advanced people; guides. Not that they will never be a guide for they often will be of course because we are all on the road to development, evolving our spiritual path. Therefore, in time we can all be guides; however, it is not often the case that a guide is a close relative that has passed recently, or even in recent past. They are around us, are concerned for us, and are protective and compassionate for us, but they are not of the status of a guide. You follow me?

People who go to your churches to give you messages, will often connect with those of your family who have passed on, for the linkage, the bond, is strong to you and they are sensitive to this linkage, sensitive to their energies. You forge links, connections, and energies with your deceased relatives and friends but this does not mean that these people are your guides. Your mediums and clairvoyants often connect more easily with your relatives and friends because of the earthly connection. However, you will have many guides and helpers around you for you do not only have one guide but may have many guides, or many helpers at least, to work with your guide.

Therefore, there are many in spirit to support each of you but you have responsibility for your own life course, your own life pattern; you who are in command, in charge of your kingdoms, (smiling) my friends, yes. We are the humble servants, so you must look upon us as advisors to the King and sometimes the King would dismiss his advisors, sometimes he would say,

"No, my friend, you have got that wrong. We will not take your advice on this occasion."

This is all well and good my friends; this is all well and good for you are the ones who are living on the earth plane, you are the ones who are in charge of your kingdom, and you are the ones who must make your decisions about your realm. It is *you*, who are responsible for your growth, not us.

Can relatives sometimes be more of a hindrance than help?

Well we would not say this but we have said before that the mere fact that we cross over into the spirit land does not make us sages, does not make us wise ones. They may be a bit wiser of course because they have learnt since they have come but this is not necessarily the case. Sometimes, interaction may occur with someone we would never have listened to while on earth because they spoke rubbish, but since coming to the spirit land they have grown fast, they have developed and they then try to influence and communicate with us and we say; 'you've got to be joking' (laughs) but this is an unfortunate turn around, yes.

How Guides and Mediums come to Work Together

One regular group member asked:

Do you choose whom to go to or are the mediums chosen for you?
It is a two way process. He (referring to the medium) was useful to us because he knew of Buddhism. I was a Buddhist monk in my former days on this earth and we choose the vehicle for communication that best befits the connection for us. So I chose him and in a sense because he had chosen Buddhism as a point of interest, he'd chosen me, or someone like me.

It is helpful for us to have someone who has a particular framework, a particular way of understanding, because if we have this it is easier for us to work with. It is still possible to work with other souls but it is more difficult and, it is as if we are trying to kick against their mental framework, for instance. We will achieve less and can less readily express our ideas. Even though we express ideas that are new and alien to Paul there is sufficient meshing of the gears, if you wish to see it this way, to facilitate our working with him, to facilitate the communication for us. Therefore, we have more going for us, you understand, than if we were working with someone who is totally alien to our way of thinking, to our way of manifesting ourselves and putting across those ideas, those concepts, those thoughts we wish to convey.

When you select a medium, does someone from the spirit land need to give you authority to use the medium, or is it a bit of a free for all?
There is an understanding but it is not like (smiling) we have to collect the piece of paper. It is not like seeking authority in your world.

If there were two spirit people on the same spiritual level and only one medium, how would you make the decision about which one would be the guide?

We would reach a conclusion to it. We would reach a conclusion based upon the ease of communication and the likelihood of the ease of the blend with the person. It would be likely that one could connect more easily than another in some aspect or other.

It is difficult work for us; you must understand this. It is not for the faint-hearted. Therefore, those spirits who are less evolved, less well meaning in their intent, soon grow tired of such attempts. They also do not have the backing of other spirits to aid them in the enterprise. For we work as a group, as a team of spirits. Without the team I would find this much more difficult so we must work as a team as you also work as teams on your side.

* * *

A circle member once asked Hai whether it was necessary for us to always go through our own spirit guides for communication or was it possible to contact any of the spirits within our group when we need to. Hai replied:

No, you may connect directly to any one of us. We are all friends together here. You must reach out to whomever you wish to reach out to. It is not a matter of protocol, (smiling) it is a matter of love, and we may reach out in love to whomever we wish without offence. There can be no offence here.

Angels

Hai was asked:
If a spirit is on a higher plane will he/she be able to have contact with the angels?
Hai laughs and says:
Angels are on lower rate, so no problem (laughter.)
He continues:
You are too attached to thinking that angels are up high. Angels are not up high; angels are spirit beings like the rest of us.

Then why are they called angels?

Because they have not had an existence on the earthly world, they exist all the time in the spiritual world. Therefore, they are angelic beings in that they do not have an earthly existence as part of their evolution in spirit. So they have a different role towards you, to act as your protectors or guides, to complement the work your other guides do.

So why do they have the privilege of being angels?

Why do you think it is a privilege? *They* might think it is a great privilege to be born on earth and have experiences of the earth plane.

Who determines what spirits do then?

The One Mind; and do not ask about its rationalisation or why one person comes to earth and one person stays in spirit for there is no answer that can be given with words.

Is it equalised?

There is no answer—that can be given with words.

Chapter 3

Ethics & Responsibilities of Mediumship

Hai has often talked to us about our responsibilities for passing on messages. One night he was asked:

How do you find the standard of mediumship?
It is variable as it has always been variable. Much concerns us. The conditions also are not ripe for you on your planet at these times. I think too much distraction. Too many (laughs) what you call, Coronation Streets (an English TV soap) so for those who wish to pursue mediumship it is hard even if their intent is firm because they are having distractions beside them while they try to engage in the enterprise. But this means also that fewer are attracted to the enterprise because of these distractions. So many people seek the good time and this is hard work this mediumship, both for you and for us.

There are complications and difficulties also. There are those who say; "Ah the spirit has given this to me so I am going to give it to you." It is like saying that the sky has showered water all over me so here is a bucket of water for you. You follow me? I will explain another way. You must take responsibility for the messages you receive. It is not that some spirit has poured this bucket of water over me so watch out here comes yours. *You* must take responsibility for the message. People passing things on do much damage sometimes and you must remember that many of the spirits that you collect in your churches and groups are no more highly evolved than when they left the earth plane. Even those who are well meaning and well intentioned may not be wise souls, and therefore, may say things without thinking. They do not understand that they may cause problems for those who receive them. So we must at all times be careful and take responsibility. You are in charge not us. You are in charge.

Someone else asked:
What would be the main piece of advice you could give us as developing mediums?

Patience—patience and endurance. You see, people come to me often and ask, what they should do. There is one person I know who wishes to become a trance medium. This person constantly thinks; what shall I do, what do I need to do? These people say to themselves; perhaps if I try this or I do that, this will be the formula. But there is no quick fix. There is no magic formula. There is a *reaching out* in openness and honesty, in well-intentioned embracing of others. But that is all you can do; reach out from your side. If you reach out from your side then assuredly we are reaching out from our side and in time will form the connection.

If you ask me for techniques that are useful to you to help you in this then you will know already I think the value of meditation. If you meditate this helps us, for in the quiet of your meditation, we are given the opportunity to slip in unawares and impress memories, images, and thoughts upon your mind. You will not always be aware of where these impressions come from but they will often have come from us.

The practice of meditation helps you when you are later engaging in more direct communication with us, when you are trying to sit and give messages, for you have already prepared and trained your mind in the discipline to great effect. But you must give what you give freely and without doubt. However, this does not contradict what I said a minute ago about also needing to take responsibility.

So for some situations, some images that you get, the image will be harmless yet may be meaningful to the person to whom you give it. You may say; "I see a man sitting in a chair." Then you describe this chair and in that simple message you have given someone evidence of someone whom they have known on the earth plane. If you say to a person, "Oh I get this feeling you have a pain in your chest!! And I see a doctor's appointment coming." What good is this; what good is this? You cannot be so sure of your communication that you can be convinced of this diagnosis, and you may in time cause much harm to the person if you've planted the seeds of fear and doubt in their heads. So it is best to leave the responsibility of the diagnosis to the doctor.

*   *   *

Jacob (our spirit mediumship teacher) also had something to say about the responsibility of mediumship. He told us:

There are many on your plane who think they have no responsibility for ethics in this part of communication. They think; if they get it, they give it. But on this principle, if you had some friends for tea and (smiling) you put some stale smelly cheese on the table for them, you would say; "Well the shopkeeper gave it to me so I am giving it to you." You follow the analogy?

You receive many visitors and messages from spirit and some of these communications are very well intentioned; some are very wise and are communications of great love and compassion. But there are other communications from less enlightened souls, from less wise souls—not that they are not well intentioned—but are less wise. Also there are those spirits who wish to give you the benefit of foretelling and this is not always appropriate.

We have already explained to you that with this foretelling there is always a risk of the medium not getting it right because you do have a degree of control over your future. Therefore, your decisions and choices of today can affect your futures of tomorrow; this is one way in which the present is intertwined with the future and indeed the present is intertwined with the past also. But for this purpose we talk of the future. Therefore, there are some souls who are too keen to foretell the future and they may come to grief in their foretelling and may cause some misfortune and suffering to those who they have given their foretelling to.

There are some souls, whom I think, must have fancied themselves as amateur doctors in their earthly life for they delight in pointing out all the afflictions that you may experience in the future. This is not good either as there can often be a complication in the interpretation of the message and so sometimes they will get that wrong. Therefore, they give the medium something which is correct but which is interpreted in an inaccurate or false way.

The crux of all this is that, *you*, when you give your communications, must take some responsibility for what you give. You are ethical beings; you are ethical souls. *We* also must be ethical souls from our side of the divide, from the spirit world. But we **all** have joint responsibility for the process of the communication. It is a three-way communication, a three-way responsibility. Therefore, the spirit who gives the communication has responsibility, you as a medium has responsibility and the person who receives the message has responsibility.

Of course the other ethical dimension to this is, as Hai has already told you; *you* are the commanders of your kingdoms. You are the kings the queens of your kingdoms. You have responsibility for your decisions and your actions, no one else. Therefore, you should not be quick to give over your 'rule' to some far off spirit in the spirit world. You understand? You can seek advice, you can seek guidance, you can seek comment, but you yourselves must take responsibility for your final actions and decisions; there are three people involved in this ethical matter, the person in spirit, you as the medium, and the person whom receives the message. So there are many strands to this, and we must therefore, all take responsibility.

*   *   *

One day we received a rather aggressive email from someone who purported to be a member of a reputable spiritual organisation. We'd been communicating with the Phoenix Group for several years and, at their request, had just started to advertise our development groups on our web site. The person suggested that we knew little about mediumship and should not be running such groups. The email continued in a rather threatening vein. We didn't want to respond in anger but it was difficult to stay calm when faced with such aggression. We decided to ask Hai for advice.

Hai told us:

We have access to understanding of these matters of development. So, it is not *you* who are relying on *your* knowledge and understanding, but *we* are assisting you, to enable you to be of some help to others in their development; in their first steps out on the road of development. There are some, who believe that they know all there is to know about these issues of development, but you have a saying; 'drop in the ocean,' yes? But there are many drops to this ocean of development and those who would pretend to know the whole ocean are in error, are deluded; for there is much to learn, much to share. Therefore, no one has the whole truth of this matter. No one in your world has all knowledge relating to this matter so you would be best to help each other as explorers, rather than thinking that any one person or group of people have already chartered all territory; are already in possession of the map. Therefore, we would advocate to you all to go forward in a spirit of brotherhood to explore this matter, for there is much to explore, much to explore.

Shall I type this up and send it back to her?

Well, you must think on this whether you wish to or not. It is your decision.

She used letters after her name, which would suggest that she was a member of a respected spiritual organisation.

Those who use such letters do not have the conviction of their own argument; do not have the conviction of the truth, for what need is there for letters, if you are convinced of the truth. What need is there of these letters; the truth speaks for itself. The truth rings a chord of truth in our hearts. Therefore, those who resort to letters, who resort to pressure, who resort to alliances, who resort to power, are in error of the truth.

We are not sure whether to let the organisation know of what she has done and we are not sure of her position.

Whatever her position, this is no way to go about things. There is no reason to go about this in this manner. We say; reach out to this person in love, in understanding. But you must put your point across also. Therefore, put your point across without malice, without defensiveness, without vehemence but in patience.

Chapter 4

Difficulties of Communication

Ego & Beliefs

The following communication started with a question to Hai about Diana Princess of Wales but then expanded into other matters concerning communication with the spirit world.

Will Princes Diana ever become a guide for someone?
Well she may in time but she is not ready yet. She is a relatively new soul over here. She has things to work through, to learn of her own account, before being ready to give to others again on your plane.
Many mediums claim to have made contact with her.
Yes well, they may well have made contact with her but this does not mean she is acting as a guide.
Do you think that ego may be interfering with some mediums over this?
Sometimes this can be a problem in that people say they have contact with so and so because they are addicted to this. They wish to experience the connection of someone of high status or of popularity. But this is not easy to tease out you know for if you have a devotion, an affection, a love of a particular person, in turn you will draw that particular person to you and if you draw that person to you there is then the possibility of communication.
So how do we know?
It is likely that if you reach out to someone they will end up standing next to you so to speak, then the question becomes, can you connect to them for the purposes of communication, and it may well be that this can happen. It might sometimes be that it does not happen and the person imagines that communication is taking place. But it is

likely that they will connect to a degree with this person because if they have a *genuine* devotion, love, for this person they will have drawn them to them. So this is not easy to resolve.

With someone like Diana I suppose she would be very busy making all this contact because she was very popular.

Yes but though they draw her to them they do so not with the intention of communication. However, those who consider themselves mediumistic then they will draw the person to themselves with the intention of communication, and therefore, the facility for creating a link is greater, is more possible.

Is there more possibility of information being clouded in situations like that?

Well there is always the possibility of information being clouded but this may come from a number of different sources. It may come from the preoccupations and assumptions of the medium's mind. It may come from assumptions of the sitters with the medium. Communication is difficult therefore, but as we have said before, in spite of all difficulties we persevere for the choice is communication with difficulties or no communication. And we believe that we shall succeed in creating and achieving significant communication that will overrule the problems of communication.

So the sitters can affect communication then, Hai?

Yes because their energy flow can intervene and affect the communication. So if they have strong assumptions, beliefs, or misconceptions these also can interfere with the flow of the communication. This is why it is important to sit with an open mind.

Eileen commented that they as a group needed to take care about their own sitters. Hai responded:

It does depend upon the purpose of communication but for best communication people should be open, receptive and attentive, but without preoccupation, without premonition of what will occur, without preference or presumption of what will occur.

*   *   *

Unfortunately we had a problem with the mini disc during the recording of the following conversation and some of Hai's answer was lost. However, we feel that his response to the question is still valid and so we decided to go ahead and print it anyway.

Hai was asked:
A lady medium told me her spirit guide had been telling her lies. Is this possible, Hai?
Hai smiles and answers:
Tell her to get them to take a lie detector.

There was some laughter and then Hai continued with:

This will depend upon what we speak about. It will depend upon what she means by being lied to. Do you wish to explain this further?
I got the impression that she was demanding too much and the answers she got back were not what she wanted to hear. She appears to be leading a very complicated life at present.

Hai began by saying:
Well there are many factors here.

The next part of the communication was lost but this is what we remember of the conversation:
Hai talked about some mediums becoming disenchanted when they do not receive certain messages when they want them and explained that this can sometimes result in them feeling that they have been lied to. The sound on the CD returned and Hai continued with:

Therefore, there are many obstacles in our way. We are gratified that you seek communication in spite of all these obstacles and we can only say to you that in spite of all these obstacles we manage from our side to convey to you what we wish in essence, to convey. Unfortunately sometimes the *details* may depart from our intent but this is inevitable in the nature of the communication process because we rely upon intermediary minds. We rely upon intermediary minds in all cases of communication no matter how direct they appear and these intermediary minds may colour, may influence, and affect, the taste of the communication. Therefore, this is always a problem for us and this is why in particular we say to you that you must always use your judgment in deciding, in weighing the messages and the evidence before your eyes. You must be the final arbitrators in what is worthy, what is worthwhile and what is not worthwhile. But in whatever form your communication takes between our world and yours there is the intermediary process and this intermediary process is fraught with problems and difficulties.

If you achieve your communication through clairvoyance you have to interpret the visual message which we give you and you may interpret this visual message in many different ways. We must, from our side, often experiment with you to see how you would interpret a particular image. And then we may have to adjust the image that we give you in order to achieve a better fit with your perceptual processes so that you may interpret our message more accurately. But there is always this problem of interpretation, yes. You agree with me my friends?

Likewise those of you who are auditory in the way in which you receive messages, even though you may actually *think* you hear words sometimes, you only hear words because we have acted on your brain in order to convey the sense of auditory sound. Therefore, in acting on your brain likewise we may encounter problems of the way in which we influence you, and therefore, even with this there can be difficulties in interpretation.

This can happen even in this present case where we use trance where in many ways we have more direct control. Nevertheless, we are acting on something in order to produce the result of something; you follow me? Like a puppet on strings you may say. Then sometimes we may pull the wrong string (laughs.) We are able to correct this to a point. So as I have said, in all forms of communication you must be cautious, you must use your own judgment. But you must not take just *one thing* in a moment in time. You must take the *broader picture* and assess on the basis of this broader picture. Does this make sense to you, my friends?

The Path of Development
Blockages to Communication

Hai was asked:

What would be the reasons why spirit would stop giving messages to a medium?

You know, it is not a progress to receive images, you merely reveal a potential, which is there already. I play with words but you see my meaning; that it is revealing what is already there, not something you have progressed to. You must know that it is a journey with your mediumship like many journeys in your life, and therefore, as with any journey, there is much winding of the route. The path may start by going down into the valley then by climbing up the hills; there is some viewing of the sights from the top of the mountain peak, and so on. So you should not expect steady, easy, constant progress. You will spend time on the plateaus consolidating what you have. You will spend time exploring the next ascent accomplishing little it would seem at the time, but while you explore the ascent you prepare yourself for it and you start off again and you see new sights, new experiences. Therefore, you should view your mediumship as a journey with all of the thrills and setbacks of a journey.

I was just wondering; if we do wrong and the messages are taken away, how can we make sure that we do right all the time so that this does not happen?

No, you do not understand. We do not take things away from you. First you must not be *attached* to the gift of mediumship; if you see it like that. If you are attached to it you will block it, you will get in the way and interfere. So the first thing is—do not be attached to it, because you need a calm mind, a fluid mind, and an easy mind to allow the flow of communication. So—I emphasise the point—you should not attach yourself to the gift. But if you are open, still and calm; this is the important thing. There are those who are too eager and their eagerness gets in the way. Therefore we will not take things away from you. It is not ours to take away in the final analysis because, as I have said before, the communication is a meeting, a blending, and a welding. You reach out to us, we reach out to you, and we meet in the middle.

You have your ups and downs in life. You fluctuate in how pure your motives are and this is natural when we are on the earth plane but you should not worry about this. You have not gone out and committed a murder have you? No. So we all fall short in small ways with our purity and intent. You should not worry about this because we are patient, we have been where you are now, and this gives us patience. You know also that we speak of our great love for you all. It is true; it is heartfelt love we feel, from the bottom of our hearts, from the bottom of our souls. So we would not take anything away from you unless you abused your gift and we, for a while, would not communicate as freely, but we do not do this lightly. It is not done often.

The questioner continued with:
I asked because a medium I know said he was shut down for three months after becoming cocky because he needed to adjust his attitude.

Two things may be happening here. It may be that he put himself in a state whereby communication was thwarted, made more difficult, but this is not necessarily spirits' doing. It may be that he put himself in a mental state, which hindered communication. If we were to take away communication from every medium that showed ego, how many people would there be left to give communication? Not many. So he may have put himself in a state, which hindered communication.

Also people at times put themselves in a state where they doubt that communication is possible. They feel they have transgressed, and if they feel they have done some wrong this will act as a block to communication. Therefore, the reasons for blockages are many and are often to be found in the human person rather than the spirit people.

We may take another example from this one (the medium) because when we started with Paul we gave many images, and many messages contained within those images. Words came with the images and we gave him vivid landscapes from my earth life. Later the development with the voice came, (smiling) 'the throat job,' as you came to call it, and the development then focused on the throat. This then distracted from the mental development with images, so the images dried up, but the images did not really dry up. He became so attuned to this way of communication that the imagery slipped into the background. We are remedying this now, you understand, but again it was more to do with his reaction to development than any reality that followed. You are superstitious people. We have all been superstitious in our time but you must relinquish superstition as far as you can because it gets in the way.

Another member commented:
People pass it down, Hai. They assume messages were taken from them for a reason and when they find themselves in a position of teaching and power they pass this information to others who also then believe it.

Hai quickly responded:
If I tell you—your glasses of water have tainted water in them—suddenly you loose your thirst. But please drink your water because there is nothing wrong with it. You take my point? There are those who have power and influence who will tell you of tainted water. Their influence carries more weight in the minds of the people and does great harm because these things play on people's minds and interfere with their lives and their freedom. It is a great pity and that's why I say you must always remain 'captains of your ship.' Do not allow anyone to override you. You make your own mind up, your own decisions. The most experienced wise person can still make mistakes.

Chapter 5

Thomas

Talking about:
Love, Acceptance, Tolerance, Blockages to Communication & Protection Issues

Thomas was not a 'founder member' of our Spirit Group, so to speak, but has communicated with us so regularly that he has become one. Thomas told us he was a slave in the cotton fields of Alabama in his last life on earth. He's often talked of those days and of how his experiences taught him forbearance. Quite often Thomas will come through to talk about a particular issue which may be prevalent at the time and which he has a particular interest in.

One night one of the circle members was concerned because of a dispute between some members of a spiritual organisation and the likely resulting effect the dispute would have on its development group. Thomas came through to offer some advice on a way forward.

After talking about the need for forgiveness and harmony within the organisation Thomas goes on to explain how disharmony can affect our mediumship.

Thomas

He told us:
You know there's got to be a forgiving on both sides. And even if there are big changes there needs to be this forgiveness because if there is not this forgiveness the sore will just carry on. Even though it does not

affect your organisation directly, even if all these folks were to go their own way, the sore would linger on in their souls, their hearts. So it's good if they can find forgiveness for each other, to make all well and to agree to recognise their own differences and just accept them, for we are all different. We should not expect us all to be the same as each other. What kind of world would that be, a mighty boring world, a mighty poor world. So we've got to learn to just accept each other in loving kindness, forbearance, and patience.

We create weight on us when we have to try to communicate in all this bitterness around the place. It locks in and interferes with the communication so if you have preconceived ideas, preconceived judgements; this can affect what will come through you from spirit. You will affect things. You will distort things.

You see, you talk about protection sometimes. I know those folks (meaning new group members) who come to you here, have spoken about protection, but the biggest protection you all need is a loving heart, an open heart, and an honest heart. For if you don't have these you can say all the prayers you like and you will not have protection. You can sit within a church within a church within a church and you will not have protection, for the only and best protection is a loving honest heart.

Circle members then went on to ask Thomas other, more general questions, about mediumship and development. One member asked:

Does my father hear me when I think about him?

You *know* he hears you, Jane. You see, you folks, you doubt. You're all what you call 'Doubting Thomas' (laughter.) As soon as you think, before you even form your thought, you have already spread out your wave of love to them, your love from here (pressing his heart area.) You already have reached through to them because it is instantaneous. The problem is more if you want to *stop* it from reaching them, than reaching them.

How do they know who it comes from, Thomas?

You have your own signature, your own vibration. It's like the wave of the sea; it's got its own signature, its own personality, and its own identity. When you send out your thought it's like a wave in the sea with its own signature, its own vibration. So it's like all these waves of the sea washing over you and they can easily identify yours.

Is it difficult for someone when they first pass over because they will receive a lot of thoughts of love, won't they?

They've got to learn that all thoughts are not of love mind. No. Some of those thoughts are not of love (laughs.)

Do they receive those thoughts as well, Thomas?

Well they might feel the thoughts of—good riddance. There are also those thoughts of grief and sadness. So you see it's a bit of an emotional storm at times.

Can you switch off from it?

Yeah you can learn to. You just pay attention to those you want to receive, and therefore, when you sort of tune in, they become stronger and clearer.

Do you actually hear the words that are formed or do you simply pick up the emotion?

No, it's like a *feeling* but it's like a *feeling that contains the words*. It's a bit like that when we try and communicate with you anyway. When we communicate with you sometimes, the words will just pop into your mind, but we do not exactly form the words in the sense of repeating them and you hearing them. It is more that we give you an impression. We impress upon you an impression, a sensation, or an image and then you get the words with it, as an intrinsic part of it.

So you do all know what we are saying then?

Oh yeah, oh yeah.

Chapter 6

A Private Sitting
Establishing a connection with the medium

The following questions came from a group of people who had a private sitting with Hai.

How do you control your medium, Hai?
We were able to link with him first because he reached out to us. In all cases we must have this intent, willingness, cooperation, this reaching out and embracing of us, in order to achieve anything with you. Whatever kind of mediumship is involved whether it is purely mental mediumship, through trance or through physical phenomena of whatever kind, we must have this reaching out from you.

We in our turn must reach towards you in order to achieve a link, a means of communication. We could speak of different forms of mediumship but you refer to trance in first instance, yes? So we were able first to make a connection with this one's aura, (the medium) and in the early days we were able to use this connection to impress images upon his mind and with these images we would convey words. But then we moved closer to him and were able to connect with his nervous system. We were able to connect with that faculty which connects with the central nervous system at a primitive level in order to express ourselves through his physical movements of his body. So we had to achieve a blending, an influencing of his physical body in order to achieve this manipulation of his physical self. This takes time. It takes time in order to achieve a sufficient blending.

It is an experiment for us as much for him for we must experiment in order to perfect our control. But though I use the word control you will appreciate that all the time we are reliant upon his ongoing cooperation. He can retract his cooperation at any time. We are dependant upon his ongoing intent and wish to work with us. We must not intrude beyond this; we must abide by his wishes, they are sacrosanct to us. But (smiling) the fact is that he and his good wife have been amenable to this enterprise and we have had much support and encouragement from those who sit with these people and so we have been able to carry on our work. However, the blending is a gradual process that must be perfected over time. There can be ups and downs with it and this is the same with all mediumship, all physical phenomena, and all patterns of communication.

The questions went on:

The Technicalities of Communication/Mediumship

So you actually use Paul's nervous system when you communicate through trance?

Yes, in order to communicate with you we must blend with his nervous system. We do not have bodies of our own; therefore, we must use your bodies. (The medium's body) We ask you to indulge us, to allow us to share with you your bodies, your nervous systems in order that we may communicate through you. You are like the electric wire, which allows the current to run through it. We are the current. The electric wire might affect the shape of the current that goes through it, to a point, and it is the same with our communication. The wire, the body, and the nervous system, which we employ with your permission, shape our energy, and therefore, it will affect the tone and nature of this communication to an extent. However, we are able to use it in such a way that we can imbue it with our message, nevertheless, and convey in essence that which we wish to communicate.

Is it the same process when someone receives messages clairvoyantly?

It is the same, but it is just that we are able to express ourselves in a fuller way sometimes through trance communication. We are able to imbue the channel, the medium, with more of ourselves, to express our nature more fully, to convey in richer tone that which we wish to communicate. But the same issues apply to those mediums who stand on your rostrums to convey mental images, which those in spirit have given them. They are still acting as channels. They are still serving as the electric wire but the blend is restricted to the imagination. It is a blending of the imagination. The medium's mind and imagination may also affect the message but again, in principle, we may be able to convey that which we wish to, to great extent.

You should however never believe that what you receive in any form of mediumship is unadulterated communication for this is not possible in the way in which communication must take place. But we are able to talk with you, to share with you, to possess the moment with you, and therefore, we are grateful for this opportunity of communion with you, which we would not otherwise have.

Are any of us developing mediums suitable to be spoken through?

It is a matter of different temperaments, of different abilities, of the correct blending to be achieved between you and the one in spirit. We may find that though someone is suitable as a channel we must find someone from our side that is able to facilitate this link and their use as a channel. Therefore, we must find someone suitable and this is not always as easy as you might think. However, once we have established the channel and one person in spirit who is able to communicate through you, then the way is laid for others in spirit to come and use you and to talk through you. And once we have some advancement, it becomes easier to develop from that point and to use the person in greater measure.

Sometimes I can feel the personality of someone very clear but other times I struggle. Is it because the person who is communicating is not blending properly?

Yes this is sometimes the case because the blending is not just one way but two ways. Therefore, if you are not as open on some occasions this may create a block from your side. But if the person on spirit side is inexperienced or is getting emotional in an unhelpful way for communication, then this may create a block on their side. So it is a matter of twofold blending coming together.

How can we on this side make it easier for the other person?

By being still. By being still—open, and receptive—not anxious, no. It is useful to send out loving thoughts first but do not hang on even to loving thoughts, for sending loving thoughts is good but then you must simply be still and open, calm and serene, like a swan on a lake.

Does that mean that all mediums should eat particular foods to strengthen their nervous system?

You are back onto your ritual again. I did not mention food. I know where you come from though.

A book I was reading suggests that mediums need to eat certain foods to strengthen their nervous system.

Why? In case they turn into some kind of skeleton? (Laughs) No it is not a serious problem and when we speak of the use of the nervous system it is mainly in the case of trance mediumship. It is rather different when we communicate through your imagination. We impress an idea there within your imagination, but we do not use the nervous system as such, in the same way. With trance the nervous system is used in much greater measure. It is not the same with mediumship of the mind. We implant ideas, visions, and images within the inner eye, and by doing this we are able to trigger the communication. But you understand that we place an image in the inner eye and by placing an image in the inner eye we cause a trigger. This causes the person to report-back on the image that they have seen.

We may also trigger other emotions through the scent of a flower but it is a similar process as with mental mediumship of images. It is like we throw a ball at a rubber wall, the rubber wall will give way to the force of ball and will show an impression of the ball. With trance mediumship it is more like we are able to put our fist in the rubber wall. This is not a particularly good analogy but you get my drift.

It is more direct in one sense. We are able to have a more direct impact through trance. Whereas we rely much more on the intermediary of a medium when we give messages clairvoyantly for they must report back on messages, must look for reactions in the other person and ask what this means to them, what does this associate for them and so on. We are able to communicate more fully, to an extent, with trance mediumship. But because it involves the nervous system and is fuller communication to an extent, it also brings limitations, for not all those in spirit are able to manipulate it to great effect. Therefore, for some it might be easier to give an impression to the mind.

I always thought it would be easy for you on your side.

No, we have our difficulties with our attempts to communicate.

Does it help if we drink pure water before meditating?

Pure water. You have a great problem these days finding your pure water, but yes, you can drink pure water. Pure water helps cleanse the system of the body. It is not a stimulant like your coffee so it is helpful to do this. Too much caffeine may stimulate the mind, may agitate the mind, not in any serious way, you understand. However, caffeine, if taken immediately prior to communication, depending upon other factors in your life at the time, depending upon your body at the time, may cause some slight agitation.

I'm never sure what to believe when I read things.

Do not believe everything you read. Even my friend, Chung Ching, agrees with me on this and he scribed my book. (Hai was referring to the book he wrote while still on the earth plane)

Part 2

Development Sessions

Chapter 7

Chan Chou

Before the Spirit Group finally settled on Jacob they sent through several other spirits who said they would help us with our development. We found each one helpful in their different ways.

Chan Chou was one of the first to offer exercises and advice. He appeared rather stern, his use of our language was quite stilted, and he started by calling each of us by a number. Nevertheless, we soon became accustomed to his manner and found his exercises and lectures very useful. Chan Chou had an amusing way of referring to the exercises he gave us as 'tricks.'

Process of Communication

Chan Chou began the communication with:

I come to aid mental imagery.

Introductions took place and some discussion followed regarding the many spirits who come to the earth plane to try and connect with our mediums but have difficulty linking. One group member asked Chan Chou:

Why is this, Chan Chou?
Sometimes the connection is not too good. It's like you tune your radio in half way but it's not quite on the right signal; therefore, you don't hear anything or you hear a garbled message. You might just hear an odd word here and there, and therefore, you give the wrong message.

What is the first thing we are aware of when someone is trying to contact us?

You become aware of a vibration. You become aware of our vibration, which you then tune into. If you can refine your tuning you will hear us well. If you cannot refine your tuning you will not hear us so well. If you are not tuned in at all you don't hear us at all. It's like a radio receiver, which you tune in.

How do we tune in?

You reach out to us, you tune in to us, and you **attune** to us. It's like you pick up a signal; you notice a signal through your subconscious, your intuition. So if you become dimly aware of a signal then you should attune to it. If you pay attention to the signal, it will come into sharper focus. As the signal comes into sharper focus the connection is made stronger, and therefore, you may communicate with us. You may receive our signals to perfection. So it is like you suddenly notice something. It is like; in your world if you see a sudden light in the corner of your eye you turn your head towards that light. Yes? And you are able to identify its source. You are able to identify its colour and its form. Therefore, you are able to perceive it to perfection because you direct your attention to it and your perception becomes clearer.

How do you know it is there in the first place?

Because it will catch the corner of your eye and this is what happens with spirit communication. It's like spirit communication catches the corner of your mind and then you suddenly realise there is something here, something there. You focus your mind on this *something* and it becomes clearer, more in focus and you become finely attuned to it.

This subconscious process is not easy to explain, or to do, but possible for if it was not possible then we could not communicate. So this is how it works in principle.

Is it easier to get communication whilst meditating?

Communication in meditation is important. Meditation aids the mind towards pitch, towards level, towards manifestation of mind. This facilitates the reception of spirit voice, spirit image, and spirit sound, and therefore, enables the mind to focus on such. Meditation helps to quieten the mind; therefore, it enables the mind to focus. Meditation can also awaken creativity and creativity is important in communication. We use the creative faculty; we use creative imagery to link to you, to relay thoughts to you, to relay images to you, which convey our thoughts.

*People get worried about the **interpretation** of the imagery.*

You'll be lucky, (joking) you get the imagery first. You can worry about interpretation when you get an image.

When we meditate and are sometimes on the verge of sleep, how do we know that the pictures we receive are not what we all get when on the verge of sleep?

Well, when on verge of sleep you may get vivid images from the spirit world because, when you are on the verge of sleep your mind is in the right state to receive images. You may go too deep of course; you may go towards sleep, in which case the dream state will take over but the dream state will produce a garbled image, an unclear image. The dream state will create an image of no consequence.

When we interpret an image, should we just go with our feeling?

Go with your gut feeling, with what you believe. But you should explain to those whom you give the message; that it is a bit like interpreting a foreign language. And you might have only studied this language up to school level but spirit talk to you at university level. So you must convey to the person, that you do your best to interpret this language but you are not up to scratch. Therefore, they must be careful with what you give them. You must tell them; it may contain the principle, it may contain the essence of what spirit say, but there may also be difficulties and some inaccuracies.

It is important to be clear to those who come to you for messages. You understand?

Exercise:
Visualisation

Chan Chou told us:

Well we will try a little 'trick' so go quiet, deep within self—deep within self, and still your mind. (Few minutes pause)

Now imagine that you put both your hands together as if holding a cup but keep hands open as if holding the cup around the sides. Now continue to imagine your hands like this until you can see a vivid image of your hands, as if your hands are there in front of your eyes, your inner eye—Slowly you see an image start to form. Continue to imagine your cupped hands and the image within your cupped hands.

The image slowly becomes more tangible; slowly becomes more tangible and clear. You start to be able to recognise the image and perceive what the image is. See this image clearly; focus on this image until you can see it very clearly, until it becomes very vivid, until you can see the detail of this image.

Notice all the detail of this image. Run your eyes up and down it. Up and down, side to side. Look at this image carefully from all angles so that you feel confident that you may describe it.

Now thank the image for coming. It will now slowly start to fade, become less tangible, less real, less solid, until it disappears. Then, mentally, slowly put down your cupped hands, which you can see in your mind's eye. Now slowly bring yourselves back, slowly come back to this room, and when you are ready, open your eyes.

The group gave feedback and Chan Chou explained:

> This meditation is an important step in facilitating mental communication. **You must practise visualisation.** You must practise **vivid** visualisation and you must practise **inner** visualisation to aid communication.
>
> Even when you believe it is your own visualisation, your own creative visualisation of your own faculty, it may be possible for us to affect and influence this and shape it to begin communication and to present what we wish to convey. So the practice of visualisation of images is important. You may cup your hands as I suggested tonight. This is not essential but you may find it helpful to cup your hands and visualise them vividly until you can see them and then see what forms within your hands. This may aid communication.

Eileen asked if it was useful to meditate while focussing on a candle. Chan Chou replied:

> It depends what you wish to do. If you wish to still your mind it may be best to imagine a candle or other such object, for this will help you to find focus. You bring your mind to 'one stop focus.' When you bring your mind to 'one stop focus' and *still* the mind, you shut up the

'chattering monkey' and when you do that then sudden insight, new insight, may come about your essence, about your identity, about reality of the world.

This though is not the way to promote spirit communication. If we seek spirit communication we must relate to *relative worlds*, not one world, one Essence, the Suchness. We rather relate to *relative worlds*; therefore, dichotomy is still present here. So if you imagine your open hands around a cup, but leave potential possibilities open and expectant, then you may receive images that may usefully bring about communication with the spirit world.

So you see this is a different level of thought, a different level of meditation if you wish, and a different level of mind is required for this. Not too deep, not too focused, but open and creative. Creative and open to being moulded, open to being shaped, to being worked upon, that we may mould, shape, create images within your mind. You understand? It is like a potter with clay. If you approach us with your open mind, it is as if we could say that your images, your thoughts, are made up of clay within your mind. Normally you shape the clay to make your ideas, your images, like you shaped your candle (referring to Eileen's feedback from the meditation.) You (referring to Eileen) shaped the clay of your mind to see a candle, but you do not act upon the clay. You do not mould the clay or work upon the clay but rather you hold it in its raw form as a ball of clay for us to mould, for us to work upon and to shape. You understand this? It is not easy to represent, but it's the best I can do.

Exercise:
Conveying a Message

Chan Chou began another exercise:

So we try another 'trick'. This time we try to convey a simple message. Go quiet and have a blank screen in front of your eyes. When you do this, a simple image will start to form. When you feel still, when you *feel* the blank screen in front of your eyes, just sit to receive. (Few minutes pause then the group gave feedback.)

Following the group's feedback, Chan Chou continued with:

> It is important **not** to try. Just be open and **do not** try or your mind will get in the way. It is also important not to come with preconceived ideas in your head. We know this is difficult to do because our heads are usually full of ideas; nevertheless, it is important to put aside these thoughts and ideas. If the 'chattering monkey' comes to meditation full of ideas, they interfere with meditation. It's not easy to get rid of the 'chattering monkey' and it's not easy to make the mind a total blank, but it is best to try.
>
> You should not come with ideas or with a sense of purpose, but truly to look at a blank screen, without purpose. If you can do this without purpose, your own mind will not interfere. Your own mind will not colour what is seen on the blank screen. We know this not easy to do but it is essential to facilitate communication. Practise makes perfect in this and all things. The more you do it, the more you are able to put your own mind to one side, the easier it will become to put aside all preconceptions, all ideas, all hopes, all wishes. For, to be successful, you must put aside all desires to do certain things and all desires to give people what they want. You must put all desires away. Only then do you have a truly blank screen on which we write.

Chan Chou finished the session by telling us that he'd given, Paul, the medium, an image of water. He explained that when a medium receives an image of water she/he needs to think not only of all the possible themes but to also take note of **anything else that comes with the water** because this can make a difference to the interpretation. In later sessions, Jacob was to expand on this theme.

Chapter 8

Jacob Session 1

The communication in the previous chapter was the only one we received from Chan Chou. We'd really appreciated the help he'd given us but it seemed that our Spirit Group were still on the look out for someone with a slightly 'better fit'. We did not have long to wait. On another night shortly after, we had our first encounter with Jacob. It seemed that the Spirit Group had 'struck gold' as we all felt immediately at home with him. Jacob's lovely relaxing manner and gentle nature helped us to relax into the sessions and we knew with certainty that he had been worth waiting for.

Some months later Hai was talking to a new female member of our group. She had asked Hai about guides. Hai answered her question and then moved on to talk about Jacob.

Hai told us:

You all have spirit guides, my friends, yes; *many* spirit guides sometimes. You may have one main guide but you may have many helpers. Spirit guides may also change during your life depending on your own need, for this is part of non-attachment. We provide ourselves and are willing to help you according to your timely need. If your need moves on and changes, then we are willing to step aside and let someone else, more fitting, help you. We do this now with your group. When we started with this group's, 'development night,' we sent through many spirits to work with you, to try things out, to see how they work with you and to find the best connection. We have tried many spirits in this way but eventually found the best person for the job, best 'fit' for you. This is not to say that other spirits are not the best 'fit' somewhere else, but for you we found Jacob, so Jacob has worked with you for many a month now.

*   *   *

Jacob
Purpose of Mediumship

The session started with some light-hearted conversation. Jacob indicated that to develop our mediumship abilities we should take notice of the monkey and observe some of his skills. He commented:

> The monkey has many characteristics which are essential for them living in the jungle and which could be of use to you. He has good vision, good hearing, and good playful energy.

Jacob went on to explain that it was important to be aware of our reasons why we want to develop and then asked us, in turn, what we wanted from the session. That night there were three of us, besides the medium, and each wanted something different. One wanted to develop spiritual awareness another wanted to be able to give messages, and the third wanted to enhance her healing skills. We decided to print the full session here, as it occurred, because three different aspects of mediumship are covered and even though the interpretations from Jacob were personal to each of us, he explained that they can have meaning and be helpful to us all.

Jacob started by asking each member of the group what they wanted from the session. When we'd each responded he explained:

> I am trying to get you to be clear about this, about what you want. For if we cannot be clear about what we wish, then this will hinder our development and this will not give us clear focus.

Below is a transcript of that session. You will see that Jacob continues to question each of the group until he is clear about what they want.

Len

I want to be a medium.
What do you mean by wanting to be a medium, Len?
Well to be able to make contact with spirit and receive messages so that I can help other people.
In what way?
I'd like to offer communication to other people.
So we have a clear focus now in terms of your development. You want to receive messages.
Yes

Janice

I would like to develop myself to become more spiritual.
So this may be done by your own practices, by your communication, assistance through spirit energies. You wish to connect with benevolent beings of spirit to help you and with your spiritual development?
Yes

Eileen

I would like to develop myself so that I become a clear channel for healing.

Jacob replied:

So we have three very different focuses for development but (Jacob smiled) you want me to do all this at once. However, I think we can find a common focus and common way forward with this. What we shall try to do is to focus upon your own 'inner guides'. For by focusing and establishing a bond and relationship with your own 'inner guides,' you may seek their assistance and develop in your several different ways.

You, Janice, may ask for spiritual development of yourself, of your own spiritual being, of your relationship to the world and others in the world, to express your spirituality towards them.

You, Len, may ask your guide, to assist you in linking with spirit beings on other planes of existence that you may connect with their minds and energies for a time, and receive a communication that you can relay to others.

You may also, my dear lady, (referring to Eileen) find a way to develop and connect with your guides, to help you become an open channel, to free any blocks that you might have and to be a conduit for your healing energy.

Contacting our Guides

Jacob explained that we must first connect with our guides. He confirmed that they were already with us, and ready to take part in the exercise. He told us to go quietly within and as we did so talked us through what he wanted each of us to concentrate on.

Exercise

We (referring to himself and the guides) would simply ask you to recognise this wish you all three have within you and to connect with your guides for your different and unselfish purposes. We will start by recognising this wish for the benefit of others. We then simply go quietly within. We deactivate our minds; we deactivate our rational conscious minds. We stop the 'monkey' babbling and we simply go within in quietness; so please go within in quietness for a few minutes. Do not become agitated. Do not expect anything—just be open, quiet, and still. (Few minutes pause, after which Jacob asked for feedback)

Len's feedback

I got the colour purple. I'm already aware of my guide and his name was coming into my mind, but I was trying to block everything else out.

Jacob responded:
Well you must not try over hard to block things out because you will cause the mind to activate and to get into a dialogue with you. So you should not try to block things out, but simply note when thoughts come to you, then let them go—let them 'drop into a pond' and disappear.

I was trying to stop everyday thoughts from coming in and just keep my mind clear.

Yes but it is better to notice when the thoughts pop up and let them then drop down again. But because you saw the colour purple, you may find that your guide is associated with this colour. So you must watch this. You must see, when you are sensing him, if this colour occurs on a regular basis. For it may be his signature for you to recognise.

So would I recognise him for his colour rather than as a being?

Yes, for when your guides come to you (referring to the group) they may give you a symbol, a colour, a shape, or something of this nature, by which you may recognise them. It is easier sometimes for them to do this, to give you an association to recognise them by rather than some other thing. They can give you a symbol that may be more vivid evidence, more concrete in your mind, in order for you to recognise them, rather than say a name or other thing. Therefore, in time you will become finely tuned and be able to recognise them from this signature. You need to practise this on a regular basis. Daily practise in this is needed but do not overdo it.

I got the name and the colour together, so does this mean he has given me both?

This shows that there is a double association and he perhaps gave you them both together to help you to recognise him. You may in time find that you are more sensitive to his energies and you may feel his energies more directly as you finely tune.

Jacob continued for the rest of us:

This is the point of this exercise, for all of you—that you finely tune your sensitivities to your guides and as you finely sensitise to their energies you find that you may become more sensitive to *them* and feel and recognise their energies more easily.

Janice

Jacob turned to Janice and asked what she'd received. Janice replied:

I was in a church. Someone who looked like Jesus was there and he had on a golden cloak. It felt benevolent and powerful.

Did he give you a gift?

No.

Jacob clearly was aware of the meaning of what Janice had received and answered:

> He gave you something. He gave you something like a cross, to bear, to take out to world. He is helping you with your love to take out to the world. Taking love out into the world is not always appreciated, not always welcomed, or recognised; yet we need people to do this. Therefore, this is about your spiritual development. But by developing yourself, your spirit, your *being* and by loving, by being compassionate, this you can then take out to the world to shine your light in the world.

(We feel Jacob was encouraging us all here to show by example, in that if we show kindness and respect for others then we are already shining our light into the world.)

Janice added:
I also saw deer running, but they were blocked and couldn't run freely.

Jacob responded:
Your guide Running Deer helps you. This image is not so much about trees and woods. He gives you a symbol of running deer. Running Deer is his name. He will help you. The running deer run free. He gives you an Indian environment, nature situation, to convey this to you. Therefore you may recognise him by this. You have other guides, other helpers also though, like the 'Christ like' figure that you saw.

This is most important for your development, for your wish to develop yourself spiritually, and to take your spirituality out to the world in free love, loving expression and compassion. To show without showing, without meaning to show your spirituality to the world. You understand me when I say this? By showing without *meaning* to show, you *be* it, you develop yourself, your spirituality, and you simply *be* towards the world. Therefore you've no need to *decide to be*. You've no need to *act to be*. You simply *are* your spirituality, for the benefit of the world. This is very good for all of us to do, but it is not easy.

Eileen

Eileen already knew her guides and she told Jacob:

> *I imagined Red Cloud and saw him take off his full headdress and put on another one with only one feather. I thought he did this because he had work to do.*

Jacob then described how *he* saw Red Cloud (in the spirit body) and explained what is required to be an open healing channel. He smiled and continued:

> The healing energy of Red Cloud is veritably pouring out of him, pouring out of him, from all of him. He is a Light Being indeed. It's like—he's so full of healing energy that more keeps coming into him but it just pours out of him. He is a *free loving channel*. He *doesn't hold on*, you see. He is a free channel; like Jesus, a free channel.

Eileen continued:
I felt myself drifting off and was going somewhere and I felt a movement to the left.
Then you recognise perhaps that they come to you from the left. This may be something that you should watch for. So if you feel a sensation from your left, you should attune to that energy for this would help them to connect with you and establish a link. This is important.

Jacob added for the rest of the group:

> You should all watch for this. If you have any sensation of them approaching you from a particular direction you should attune to that direction and you will help the bond. It's like as I said about colour and so on, by attuning, paying attention to colour, or whatever else they use, you assist the bond. But also if you are sensing energy from them, from whatever direction, if you attune yourself, if you pay attention in yourself to these things, then you are aiding the connection and the bond. So this is fine-tuning, and, patience, calmness, and stillness are very important for this development to work well.

Exercise:
Asking our guides to assist us with our development

Jacob had a different purpose in mind for this exercise and he again gave each of us specific instructions. He began:

> We go within again to meet our guides but this time we are going to ask them to assist us with our own particular purpose for our development.
>
> Len, I want you to ask your guide to convey some message to one of the people present here. You will go within and make your mind a 'blank slate,' in stillness and you will see what comes.
>
> Janice, you will please do the same, but you will go within and ask your guide to give you some deep philosophy, some deep message of comfort or spirituality, to assist people to understand and live their lives. So you are asking for some philosophical guidance of some sort.
>
> Eileen, you will connect to Red Cloud. Imagine him as a 'being of light' that healing energy is veritably spilling out of. You will ask him for some insight to do with healing.
>
> Do not worry about any of this because it is all an experiment. We are in the early days of experiment so you must just give what comes. So please go within and connect with your guides. (Few minutes pause)

Feedback

Len

Len got the colour purple and the name of his wife's Aunt. He had seen her (clairvoyantly) tending a geranium from a window box and had received the impression that she could still watch over her niece and Len even when doing other things. Jacob commented:

> She gives you this image to show that she has a good vantage point ⁓use she is tending her window box high up. Even while tending ⁓en she can still come and be with you both. She is with both of ⁓ two are one and she is here for both of you.

Janice

Janice said she'd got a strong impression of the sun, which can affect all of us on the earthly plane. She also received a flower with an eye, which was looking at her but added that she also was looking at the flower. Jacob commented:

> Ah this is good. You must develop this interpretation of the flower. It is a Oneness of life but not in an abstract way, not in a philosophical way, but in an experience way, a heart way. You look at the flower and see it with your eye and you feel that the flower sees you, so there is a bond, a harmony, a sense of Oneness and togetherness. So you are speaking here of the Oneness of life but the Oneness of life in the deepest sense possible, of the Oneness truly of heart, of spirit, of mind, of Oneness. So it's a beautiful image you get, an image that we can all reflect on, that we are not alone, we are not separate. We are all joined together in a Oneness, a beautiful Oneness of heart and Mind Being. It is a beautiful, beautiful image. So when we touch a flower, we touch ourselves, so close is the connectedness between a flower and ourselves. Yet how many would pick up a flower without giving it a second thought, without thinking of it in this way.

Eileen

Eileen had seen her guide, Red Cloud in a yellow light. Jacob's only comment was:

> Healing energy colour.

Eileen also got a slight pull to the left and Red Cloud seemed to be holding up a gold trophy. She said that she got the feeling that he was telling her it was ok to accept a small gift for healing. Jacob replied:

> This was a good message because a gift given in loving compassion should be accepted. There is nothing wrong in accepting if someone wants to give you gift out of love, compassion, and appreciation. There is nothing wrong in this. It completes a circle you see. You give, they may want to give, and this is fine and completes the bond. (This was

an interesting interpretation given that, at that time, Eileen had great difficulty in accepting payment for healing)

Jacob told us that we'd done enough exercises for one night but before he ended the session. He told us:

> We have done well tonight but this is enough for now. I would encourage you to work at your exercises. I think if you practise daily, you will find further development.
> *Will the guides always come in from the same side?*
> They will usually come from that side. You will grow sensitive to their energies as they approach you. You will feel their energies more strongly as you attune and develop your sensitivity towards them. This will happen. You do not need to spend a long time at it, just ten minutes perhaps, when you are able to get some free time to yourself in the quiet with no distractions or noise. You are then able to go within and see what comes. You would be well to write down what you get for your own benefit.

Note: You can read another communication on contacting your guide later in this section.

Chapter 9

Jacob Session 2

Different forms of communication

This was our second session with Jacob and after the usual pleasantries he indicated that it was time to get down to some work. Jacob's light-hearted banter continued as he referred to our exercises as 'games'. We have not printed the entire communication here but we felt that the following section, where Jacob describes the various different forms of communication and some of the potential difficulties when developing, could be useful to anyone developing mediumship.

Clairaudience: *faculty of hearing spirit*

Jacob began by telling us:

> So as with all of these things, all of these 'games' that we play, we must enter into the inner quietness. We shall play some games tonight which will encourage us to try to think about and to focus upon, energies around us; communicative energies from the spirit world, which we will try to connect with, in a variety of ways and forms. This is the enterprise for tonight my friends.
>
> This is not so different from what we did last week but we shall try a different tack. So you must be patient with me and we will see what we can do. It is all of course experimental, an experiment that is likely to have greater fruition if you practise regularly. (Smiling) So I give no guarantees unless you practise regularly.
>
> So we shall first try to focus using the faculty of hearing but we must first go deep within ourselves. We must try to lose ourselves in our inner stillness. So let us go within and find our inner peace, our

inner centre. This will take a few minutes. When you have achieved this, I will speak to you again while you are in your inner stillness, and you will not be bothered by my voice. You will simply listen to my voice and be guided in the direction that I wish you to go. (Jacob left us in our silence for about one and a half minutes and continued)

Well my friends you are in your inner stillness, your inner quiet. I would now ask you to listen, to simply listen, and to focus your energies on your faculty of hearing and without expecting anything, wanting anything or seeking anything, listen attentively with your faculty of hearing. Let your faculty of hearing be open, be open to a message, of words and impulses. So we will sit quietly for another minute and simply be attentive and see what comes. (There was a two minutes pause and Jacob continued)

I will ask you now to come round to your everyday consciousness; quietly return to your everyday consciousness and the room in which we sit.

After a minute or two Jacob continued:

Well now you are back so we will see if you got anything, but I do believe it is not ideal circumstances for this practise.

The group did not feel they had done particularly well with this exercise. Everyone gave feedback and then Jacob had the following to say about the development of clairaudience:

Well we have had some success but I would say to you there are difficulties with this, which is inevitable in the early stages of the development of clairaudience. When you go quiet and I tell you to focus on your faculty of hearing, you take it too literally and so when I tell you to focus on your faculty of hearing **you do precisely that** and you are hyper sensitised to every sound you hear around the room and outside.

Now, when you are skilled at going 'within,' when you have found your inner quiet, your inner stillness, what happens is that your mind is withdrawn from your external environment and it is focused inside. Then you focus with your hearing faculty rather than your ears and when you focus *inside* with your hearing faculty it is not bothered by the one-thousand-and-one distractions outside, for you are listening *within*.

Nevertheless, we have had some success tonight. I would say though that this particular development is best conducted in a totally quiet room, (with amusement) sealed even to prevent intrusion of noise and sound. But as I say, as you become more skilled and practised in this you will find the sounds around you are not a problem, for you will be able to retreat into your inner silence, and even though I would say to you 'listen' I mean you should listen *within* that capsule of inner silence. Do you understand me? But this takes time; you have heard of those monks who would sit in meditation beside a waterfall and they would become so practised at their meditation that they could not hear the sound of the waterfall. This is truly entering into an inner quiet, an inner stillness.

Clairsentience: *feeling/sensing spirit*

Following on from our exercise on developing clairaudience, Jacob indicated that he would now like to try a 'feeling' experiment but before going on to this exercise he gave us some insight into how different forms of communication work. He told us:

As you know there are three main faculties for receiving messages, three main faculties, processes, avenues, if you like. One of these is through the hearing, the auditory faculty, and another is sight. But when I use these terms of course I am not talking about physical sight or physical hearing. I am talking about the *inner* faculty. It might be that sometimes people might actually *see* with what they think is their physical eye, but it is not necessarily so. What is happening is that a spirit is connecting with their visual faculty and in connecting with their visual faculty inside their mind, their brain; they may project their image outside, but it does not mean that the person is actually stood over there.

So we may *see* things through our 'mind's eye,' we may *hear* things through our 'mind's ear,' we may also *feel* things through our sensitivity of 'feeling.' And again I do not necessarily mean here *literally* touch, though some may apparently feel something more concrete. But I mean more a feeling, an intuition, and an inner awareness of someone or something being near. Like as if it comes near or touches our aura. You understand?

Exercise:

Jacob told us:
We will try this next exercise to focus upon the faculty of 'feeling' and 'sensitivity.' We will try to make ourselves aware of energies which may be around us, and which create a feeling of difference in our own aura, our own sensitivity area. So once more I would ask you to go deep within your inner stillness, inner calm and quietness. I will speak to you again when you are all there. (Jacob left us for a few minutes and continued)

Well my friends you are within your inner stillness, your inner quiet. I would now ask you to simply sit in the stillness. This time, rather than focus upon the mind's eye and receiving things of vision, or focusing upon the hearing faculty to receive sounds or messages in this form, I would ask you simply to sit, to sit in sensitivity and awareness to any change in energies, or energies which may come near you, or feel you, or touch you in any way.

The group gave feedback and one member explained that the only thing she had felt was a touch to her throat at the very beginning. She wondered whether this was relevant. Jacob, made the following comments:

Well it might be, that as you were just dipping into yourself, just dipping into the quietness and stillness, you were most responsive to feeling energy, to touch, to communication, because we sometimes find that we are responsive at certain points in the process. Some would find they are at the peak of the potential, the possibility of communication, when they are just going into their inner quietness. Some find when they are deep within their inner quietness the communication comes. And others find that just on the up-turn, the return to full consciousness that the communication comes through at that point. So you see, we all vary. We must not, therefore, be influenced over-much by the experiences of others because this could throw us. If we expect our experiences to be the same as others, we are putting ourselves in their mould. This may not be helpful for it may not be our way of working, for us as a person.

Before we moved on Jacob was asked:

Is clairsentience, perception?

Yes, it is a subtle thing this perception, this feeling, sensing. It is like—you *know* but you do not know why you know. It is like—you get a message but you do not hear it, you do not see it, and yet you know it. It is the most subtle of the ways of perceiving and connecting to us so it is sometimes the most difficult to develop, but it can be strong, it can be good and true; as clear as any other way of doing it.

In all these different ways of development it can happen of course that sometimes you will connect and it is like—all the switches are firing off at once. But we would say you must be careful to guard against this with this sensing approach. When you get a sense of vibration, a sense of *something*, you must try to (smiling) tune in the 'radio' to that particular station. This I know is difficult to do, but if you *feel* the message of the vibration, you will feel the way to tune to it. You may not always get it right at first, but as you practise, you will be able to tune into the vibration, more expertly. It is important to try to focus in that way because if you do not and you end up firing on all cylinders at once, then it becomes confusing, perhaps more confusing than the soul who sees hundreds of faces all at once. So it is a matter of practise.

Is there a special exercise for this Jacob?

Yes you can just sit back in your chair and you can just let your *senses* or *feeling*, be responsive and receptive. You can do this in the comfort of your own home. We know there are some who would caution you about being open to spirits in this way. We would say that, because you have your heart in the right place you would be taken care of. But if you find it helpful, you can reach out before you do this exercise and tell the spirits that are around you; that you welcome those who are well intentioned. You do not need to say anything more because by definition those (laughing) who are not benevolent are not welcome. But if you have a good heart and good intention when reaching out, then this will take care of everything anyway.

Jacob then took us through our third exercise, which he believed was the easiest of the three:

Clairvoyance: (Imagery) Exercise

Jacob began with:

> This time we will try the easiest. We will focus upon the imagery. We will focus upon the faculty of inner vision. This generally, people find the easiest, though not always so.
> And so I will ask you to go within and this time to be receptive to images that you may get. Sometimes people find it helpful to imagine a blank screen in front of their inner eye. Others find it helpful to simply let their mind be still and the images will pop in. It is up to you to find the best way of doing this and you may find it useful to experiment in different ways. You may also wish to try some of the techniques that we have given you on other occasions, like one of our friends (another spirit) invited you to imagine a crystal ball so that things could form within it or could emerge out of a fog or a cloud. It is entirely up to you to experiment with these devices, to find which one suits you the best. It may be in the long term you do not need them anyway and that images will simply pop into your mind. However, they can often be helpful in the early stages, so we leave it to you to decide what you wish to do here. In the meantime, I suggest that you go inside your inner stillness, to achieve that tranquillity which is so important to us if we are to connect with you. So let us please once more return to our inner stillness.

Jacob left us for one and a half minutes then continued:

> My friends I would ask you to simply sit and wait, to await an image by means of which a message may be communicated to you.

After a further two minutes pause the group gave feedback. This time the entire group had received something. Jacob gave each member of the group assistance to interpret what they'd received, then before finishing for the night, he gave us his final comments.

You must experiment my friends and find those devices that work for you. Do not be railroaded or strait jacketed by other folk who have found *their* way, *other* way but which is not necessarily *your* way. Yes, you understand me? So I leave that with you and take my leave tonight.

Chapter 10

Jacob Session 3

Problems that can occur during the Process of Communication

This was our third session with Jacob. Hai spoke to us for some time, then, while we were waiting for Jacob, one member commented upon another development circle where there had been a constant change of membership. She commented that this often caused difficulties in the communication process. Jacob came through at the end of this conversation and commented:

I will pick up on this little theme that you have provided me with—this changing of faces, this changing of connections. It is an interesting theme to pick up. For as you imply, new faces, new connections, new energies in your group may cause us (referring to the spirits who communicate) some degree of confusion, because if we are not well connected with you, the energies change, the faces change, the feelings change, and therefore, this in some way can inhibit communication.

Therefore, we would say that this is often a problem with communication with the spirit world for there can be all kinds of misconnections, you understand. So, for instance, it might be that you will 'see;' for example, someone's grandmother and you offer a message to the person about the grandmother, and then all of a sudden the exchange switches and you find yourself talking to the person's grand*father* but he has 'come in' almost unnoticed by you. So one minute his grandmother is talking to you about doing the laundry and the next minute his grandfather is talking to you about digging the garden, and this is most confusing.

This can happen when you are communicating with the spirit world because it is like—you have lots of multiple connections. If we use the example again of the grandmother and grandfather; it is as if you have the potential to connect with a whole number of different spirits and you throw the switch in one direction, or sometimes it feels like the switch throws itself in one direction, and you end up talking to the grandmother. Then for some reason or other a short circuit occurs, the switch clicks and you find yourself connected to the grand*father*. But this switch sometimes goes unrecognised by you, for it happens so subtly, without you noticing. Therefore, you can find yourself on a different wavelength literally without the full awareness of what has transpired.

This is the difficulty when communicating with the spirit world. It is not an exact science. Neither is it, from your side, or from our side, a matter that we have total control over. It is an evolving science, not easy to manipulate or to control.

So you must bear this in mind when you are undertaking communication. You must bear with the difficulties, which we in turn also have to bear with. We must work with what we've got. We must work with what we can and do our best with it. So we shall now try a little experiment.

*   *   *

A Set of Exercises

Jacob gave us the following three exercises. We've printed them one after the other followed by Jacob's comments.

Exercise:
Meeting Someone from The Spirit Realms

When you are ready, close your eyes and go within. I wish you to imagine yourself on a seashore, a seashore at night with darkness all around you, but through the darkness you can see the beautiful silvery moon hanging over the horizon far out to sea. There is a light mist, over the sea, which seems to enhance the beauty of the moon that shines through it.

So I would ask you my friends to form this image in your minds for a minute or two, a strong image where you are stood on the shore line of a beautiful sea at night with mist stacking over water, the beautiful silvery moon lighting all, shining through the mist. I would ask you to hold this image for a while, my friends, and as you hold this image, let the mist swirl, and form; therefore, we may see a being, a spirit come out of the mist. (Jacob left us for two or three minutes before asking us to open our eyes)

Group Exercise:
The Crystal Ball

The following exercise was done as a group and there is no doubt that having the person close by does help to connect to the energy of that person. However, it may work just as well if you sit on your own and visualise the face of the person you are trying to obtain a message for. Why don't you try it and see.

Jacob began:
    Please go quietly within. Close your eyes. This time I want you to imagine, in your mind's eye, a great big crystal ball. This crystal ball is so big it occupies all your vision, your 'inner eye.' So you must fix this in your mind's eye, so you get a good picture of it. Then I want you to pick the face of one person in this room and imagine the face of this person in the crystal ball, just like it is reflected in the crystal ball. Simply focus upon this image and see what comes. (We were left for two or three minutes before being called back)

Exercise:
Symbolism & Interpreting Communication

This time I want you to imagine that you are holding a mirror in front of your face. You can see your image clearly in the mirror but it is as if there is a light haze over it. Now, look through the light haze at your face, and see what else comes. (Two or three minutes pause)

Questions

After the last exercise one group member commented that she had found the earlier exercise easier because she'd been able to focus on a particular person. Jacob responded:

> This is generally the case, in that you can focus on the energy of a person and then you can try to connect with them more closely, and as you connect you will find that you will receive some message. You've got to do it subtly, quietly, and calmly. This connection with energy is a subtle process. But as you connect with it you will find that another impression comes to you, which you may then convey to the person. But you must be sensitive to the subtleties of the message. You may find that it is *very* subtle but you must try to pay attention to the subtle changes within the impressions that you receive. Then you will find that you will get some message.

What do you mean when you refer to the changes, Jacob?

> Well you may find for instance that you get an image of someone and then you focus on that image but you find that it's already changed in a subtle way. So, it may be that you see the person before you as you would with your physical eye, then all of a sudden they are wearing glasses, so the glasses have got some special meaning because they weren't there before. In other words—they've come 'out of the blue.'
>
> Therefore, you know that this must make some significant message for you to convey to them. So you must be aware of subtle **changes** in the impression you get because these changes may be of help to you. This can apply to other things too. When you get an image of, something physical; for example, a bridge, or something else and you find that faces appear on the bridge or the bridge becomes decrepit, old, broken, or it takes on a different colour or something of this nature. You may find that this also will be significant.
>
> So it is best to 'speak' it as you see it and then you will find that, as you go with the flow, as you 'say' it to the person, you may find that an impression of significant interpretation comes to you. But it is important to go with the flow of it, to imbue yourself in the representation that you have received. By doing that you blend yourself with the energy, with the impression, which you've received, and you may find that it will develop for you. It may grow as you talk.

So you tell the person as you see it?

Yes, as you see it and talk about it, you may find other impressions, other things, come to your thoughts and then you can say that too, and so it grows. Remember **speaking** helps to connect you to the link. And as well as helping to establish the connection more strongly, it is reassurance for us, on this side, of what you are receiving. So it is helpful from that point of view, when giving someone a message, to allow the communication to flow like that and connect yourself with the energy, with us, and as the connection grows the images may grow. Messages that you receive may grow also.

So when we say exactly what we get, that makes it helpful for your side does it?

Yes, because by saying what you receive **as you see it**, you are re-enforcing the connection with us. You are keeping the line open so to speak, so it is helpful, both to us and to you, in establishing the connection more strongly.

Note:
Please bear in mind, when acting upon Jacob's advice above, he is not advocating here that we suspend our responsibility when passing on information that could cause the recipient concern i.e. we do not pass on information that we feel could be harmful just because 'spirit' has given it. Jacob was simply offering guidance on how we can encourage spirit communication to flow.

Ethics and responsibility in mediumship are covered in Chapter 3 and elsewhere throughout this book.

Chapter 11

Jacob Session 4

In the first exercise below, Jacob begins by taking us into our stillness and asking us to imagine a pond with ripples. He then talks us through a visualisation where the pond becomes calmer. You may find it useful to record this exercise onto a tape or mini disc then you can play it back as you go within to your stillness.

After the second exercise, Jacob attempts to explain, by imagery, how spirits give messages and following the third exercise, Jacob emphasises how we must use judgment when we receive messages from spirit.

Exercise:
Stilling the Mind and Meeting a Loved One

Jacob began the session by telling us:

> Well I think we will try to connect with a loved one in spirit tonight. So I would like you to go quietly within. I want you to make your minds go blank and still, like a quiet pond. Now imagine this pond in your mind's eye and first you will find there are ripples on it that are caused by your thoughts. Your thoughts are like the ripples of wind, which shake up the waters. I ask you to concentrate on this pond and on its surface. As you concentrate on its surface you will find it will go stiller and stiller. If your mind should generate some thoughts then just note the thought and let it go, let if drift away and return to watching the pond. You will then find it goes stiller and stiller. So I would like you to practise this for a few minutes until you have

achieved a quiet surface on your pond. (Jacob left us for a few minutes and then began to talk again while we were in the stillness)

My friends, if you have your quiet pond I would ask you to let go of that also. Let it recede out of your sight until your mind is just a limpid pool itself, until your mind is just quietness. Out of this quietness you will find that an image will start to form. Allow it to take shape, to become solid in your 'inner eye.' As it forms in your 'inner eye,' hold on to this image and bring it back with you to this room. So gradually, gradually return to your physical senses and bring with you the image, which you have seen in your mind's eye.

The group gave feedback then Jacob took us through the second exercise of the night.

Group Exercise:
Giving a message to another person

Jacob told us:

This time I want you to focus on the person to your right. I want you to give out an intention. I want you to think of a need, which this person has, that can be answered and which you can find a helpful answer for. Send out the intent, and ask—if this person has a need and I can be a channel for a message to answer that need, then please let it be so. Then just allow whatever comes to come.

So go within and just quieten your minds. When you are at the right point, send out your intent and then just go quiet and see what comes. (Few minutes pause)

How Spirit Give Messages

The group gave feedback and Jacob asked if we had any questions. One person commented:

I find it difficult if we are told who to concentrate on. I would prefer to wait and spirit to choose.

Jacob smiled and replied:

What makes you think spirit chooses the person? This is a massive assumption you know, Jane. What is happening is that when you are told who to focus upon, your mind is set on the task, and because you feel you are given a task to do, your mind becomes agitated, unsettled, and therefore, this causes ripples on the 'pond' again. But if you find it easier when not directed to a particular person it is not so much that you, as you say, allow spirit to choose, it is more that you are in a state of quiet stillness and you are open to receiving the vibration. So it is partly that *you* reach out and partly *them* reaching out to you. It is a meeting in the middle. It is not that the spirits say—"Oh there is Jane, we'll try her." It is not like that. Communication occurs because **you reach out** and this is why a calm mind is important. You have a number of spirits reaching to you and you connect because the connection is good with one soul rather than another soul.

I get tense because I worry that I won't receive anything.

Yes well this is why I say that *you* give yourself the task. It is better when you are not under pressure because then you can let things happen more naturally but as soon as you try to connect with a particular person you give yourself a task, a performance to achieve. It does not matter if you try to connect to a particular person and there is no performance to achieve because your mind will stay calm and relaxed. So just experiment and if it happens that's ok but if not, it's no big deal.

When you are put on the spot your mind will get agitated and this can be difficult sometimes. You see, the person who is experienced in platform work may perhaps more easily find a way of doing this because they are relaxed, well practised, well rehearsed, more natural etc. So they are able to go into a restful state and still make connections with spirit folk. So peace of mind is important in all this. It's not helpful if you are put too much on the spot especially when you are developing in the early times. It is inhibiting.

How do spirit actually give us the messages?

Well it is like this: I will give you imagery: If you can imagine yourself as the layer of sand on the beach, but just below the surface where you cannot see. Do you understand me so far? So you are just below the surface of the beach, all dark, can't see, but you can *sense* things. You sense the vibrations of the little crabs that travel over you. You sense the feet of the people who walk across, thump, thump, yes? Then one day someone comes to your little spot on the beach and they take their finger and they draw in the sand. And as they draw in the sand you *feel* and say; oh, oh yes well that feels like a z and I'm not sure what that was but this feels like a picture of something, a horse perhaps, yes, and then, ah the sea has come in again—picture gone. You follow me?

I try to convey to you the difficulty of all this. It is one-step-removed communication. We try to imprint things on your mind, your thoughts or in your hearing, but we cannot be one-hundred-percent sure that what we convey will be what you receive and that you will interpret it correctly. So this is a difficult enterprise. Yet we persist because we believe the endeavour is worthwhile and because some communication between our two worlds is better than none.

So never accept from anybody, "ah your grandfather says this." No, you may listen, but then ask yourself; "well would grandfather say that. Is that typical of grandfather? Is it good advice also?" Do not take it as gospel.

In spite of all these difficulties you will get some evidence of survival, little snippets here and there. This we must be content with, for when we are able to convey more detailed messages, and we do it correctly, it comes over with validity. But it is no easy process. Anyone who pretends it is an easy process deceives themselves and others. They may be overconfident and I am not saying they do this deliberately, but they may be overconfident in what they get and how they interpret what they get.

So we must proceed with the experiment between our two worlds. We experiment from our side and you experiment from your side. Hopefully the chemistry works in the middle and the experiment works to a point. But most experiments do not work one-hundred-percent, do they? So we must be content if they work some of the time.

I heard that there is a physical place in our brain where we meet spirit, is that so?

Yes there is a physical place within your brain, as you say, that is sensitive to communication. In fact there is more than one place for we can use these chakras that you talk about, but you must still acknowledge that the communication is by remote control. It is a manipulation. It is a tampering. It is like playing the piano. You do not get inside and pluck; you play the piano on keys and create music by remote control. This is similar to message giving but message giving is not as precise.

It is like—we are all *here* you see (in the room) and we are able to make a connection with his (the medium's) primitive brain and we are able to play the piano. And what you see is the result, which is not without merit. We get some good results from this playing the piano. However, it does not quite work all the time, but we get quite a lot.

As you improve working with the medium, is it you that's improving or the medium that's improving?

We are both improving. We are rather improving the connection and how it works. This is what is happening. We 'tinker' with it like a computer connection.

Using Judgment over Messages/Communications

The questions continued in a new vein:

When we wake in the middle of the night and receive pictures, are they messages for us or someone else?

Well this can vary. At times we are connecting with a deeper level of consciousness, of spirit. We are sometimes able to see the future or 'a maybe,' at least. At other times we are connecting with our own deeper true selves and we are given a message to meet a need perhaps. We can also receive a message in this way about our needs, hopes, aspirations, and our needs for development. We may also tune into other things that are going on in this world and find our messages from this. So it varies depending upon what we get because fundamentally we are putting ourselves in a state of mind where we are open to receiving more wavelengths. Therefore, we sense and gain a vibration, which enables us to receive some messages.

*   *   *

One person told Jacob about a picture she'd received in the early hours of the morning. Jacob helped interpret the picture and went on to say:

It is important to acknowledge when you do hear spirit talking to you or calling your name because sometimes they get disheartened and need their confidence bolstering.

But I thought you all, knew everything.

No, no, this is not the case. You must be careful of the 'passers by' when you have your communication sessions in your circles. You get people passing through, dropping in, and 'giving the benefit.' But is what they say always of benefit, this is the question. Many good hearted souls visit you and try to convey to you something of merit but there are always some in the crowd that, 'slip in,' like you had recently at Prince William's party, (reference to the interloper at his eighteenth birthday party) so you have spirit interlopers sometimes at your circles.

Are you saying that we shouldn't take too much notice of the messages we get?

No I'm not saying that. I just mean be careful, for there are occasional interlopers. You've got to use your judgement. You must not go to your groups, even this one, believing that everything you hear is gospel.

Circle leaders often say we are protected in the circle, especially if it is held in a church.

You can be assured that you will get the odd interlopers there, as you will anywhere else.

*   *   *

We'd had a few weeks break between this session and the last and Jacob finished by explaining the purpose of the night's communication:

The purpose of tonight is to recap. Next time we will move on. So practise and make a mental note of what you experience. You may write it down if you wish.

Jacob, always keen to attract more people and bring in humour, continued:

We must find some way to reach out further than your circle of friends. You can reach out on your Internet also. You can put some of these exercises on your website. You do not need to do them all because I do not feel it will be useful to put too much out at one go. But just something small for people to try out, then they can come back and ask questions and (smiling) I can go on the web board and answer them. If we really get it going well with the computer we can put the messages on the message board ourselves. (Laughs) No I do not think so, but a nice idea.

But the group hadn't finished with Jacob yet so the questions continued:

Is there anything we can put in the room to help communication?
Yes they like flowers of course. They like some scents but you must be careful that they are not too intrusive and that you can identify them easily, because if we want to create *another* scent, you must be able to distinguish it clearly. But it is nice to have a gentle perfume that is not obtrusive and which is clear. Not potpourri, which is full of all kinds of smells. It is nice to have pleasant pictures around also.

Can you actually smell flowers?
We smell the vibration of the flowers; beautiful flowers and we bring our own flowers with us. So you bring flowers and we bring flowers. You bring your flowers and you hope for communication and we bring our flowers and we hope that you will have some awareness, some appreciation, and some sense of the gift.

Chapter 12

Jacob Session 5

In the session below Jacob tried something new. We've printed some of the group's feedback here because we think Jacob's answers amply demonstrate the various connotations that apply when interpreting messages.

Group Exercise:
Using the 'Third Eye' & Psychometry

Jacob first asked us to pass some item of ours to the next person. He then continued:

> Close your eyes and hold your article firmly but gently. We would ask you to focus your 'third eye', your mind, upon this article—like you would connect your 'third eye' with the energy of the object you hold. There should be a Oneness, a Connectedness between your 'third eye' and the object that you are focusing upon, so there is no difference between the two. There should be a communion between this object and your mind. You must aim for this first, and you may gently rub the article if it helps you to focus upon it.
> I now want you to reach out to a spiritual link, and therefore, to put your mind into a state, a vibration which is reaching to the spiritual rather than the things of this earth. Therefore, my friends, if you just continue and concentrate in this way for a few minutes; we shall see what comes.

Feedback:
Interpretation of Symbolism

One member of the group, Carol, had found herself looking into a shop window and saw a group of dolls. She had focused upon one of these dolls. She also got a picture of a grandmother figure. Jane, the person whom Carol had focused upon, confirmed that an aunt, when on the earth plane, had once given her a doll.

Jacob's comments:

> You see we spirits are what you would call (smiling)—not very skilled at communication. We have to find ways of conveying our thoughts and our emotions to you; therefore, we may give you a whole shop window of dolls when all we want to convey is *a* doll. We may do all kinds of things to convey something that we wish to convey to you because we just have to connect with you in any way possible to convey our central idea. This is only one example but there are many.
>
> I asked you also to connect with the spiritual vibration of the object you held because it is a bit like, what you would call, 'riding the waves.' It is like; if you hold Jane's watch you could go 'riding the waves' in many different directions. So because the watch is close to Jane's physical vibration, you could go 'riding the waves' on her physical life, her memories, her physical vibrations. But also this watch is connected with Jane's spiritual self, and therefore, it connects with that too, and so you go 'riding the waves' in a different direction.
>
> And so, Carol, you've got to be a skilful surfer, you see, because if you ride your surfboard in that direction, you go off in that direction. If you ride it in the other direction, you go off in that direction, and so on. *So this is why I ask you to put a spiritual focus in your minds upon the object,* to encourage and facilitate a direction, which is more of a spiritual link. All things are spiritual in the final analysis but we wish to make a connection with the spiritual world on this occasion, so I asked you to think of a *spiritual* focus, to give a spiritual emphasis to your thought.

Jacob added that he didn't know whether he had explained it clearly enough and continued:

This is a difficult thing for you because we give Carol a whole shop of toys and she thinks; "What am I supposed to make of this?" But the key thing is that, it is *toys*. So we latch on to that central idea and if we see a doll in the window then we focus upon the doll, because that is the most significant thing. But on another occasion you might find that this doll is clothed in a certain way and you are particularly drawn to the dress of this doll. For example, it might be of a particular kind of material. Therefore, on this occasion it might be that it is the *dress*, that is important, but the spirit has used the idea of the doll just to let you 'ride the wave' and the story the spirit might want you to convey could be the *dress* because the dress might be significant in another way.

So you have to try and interpret as best you can what your spirit friends are trying to convey to you. If you do not get it right the first time you should not worry too much because they will probably try another way, and then another way, before they get fed up (laughter.) But this is the nature of it and there is no easy way. There is no, what you call, 'quick fix.' It is not like you talking to each other on this planet where you can speak directly, and even when you speak directly it is not always so easy is it, because you still have misunderstandings and misconceptions. So it is much more difficult for us when we are trying to reach your 'third eye', your mind, in order to convey messages. The visual communication is very rich, but it is also difficult because it is open to many interpretations, and so we have to feel our way more.

Jacob then referred to 'idea grams' and indicated that Hai had told him that his own language (ancient Chinese) was rich in meaning but apparently was also difficult because it was open to many interpretations. Jacob continued:

So it is difficult, therefore, to convey a precise meaning when you are talking to other people with 'Chinese on paper' and it is similar to that. Therefore you have a difficult time, my friends, in reaching us, in reaching the image and in interpreting these images, but please do try, do not lose heart, do not become discouraged. We rely upon you to have a go, just like we have a go, because we have also a responsibility from our side to try our best to convey to you an appropriate image.

Carol asked if her vision of Jane looking longingly in the window meant that she would get whatever she wanted? Jacob expanded on his previous reply:

> There is a possibility that when we receive an image, we focus upon it and *our mind gets to work on it* and this is another difficulty. But when you get an image and you get a *gut* feeling about this image; you get a sense of urgency to get it out. Now that is probably the communication at its safest, at its best, at its clearest. The difficulty is that we have minds. We have minds for a purpose because we need our minds to talk to each other and so on. However, the difficulty is that when we receive an image, a concept, from the spirit world, there is a danger of our own minds getting to work on it and interpreting it.
> Now this may be ok to a point, but we've got to be careful, because the mind is a wonderful little 'mad monkey' and it goes off in all kinds of directions. So we've got to be a little bit careful about attaching too much significance to some things in our scenes. Now the most important thing that you received here was the spirit wanting to make a connection and to do this she brought a memory. She wished to demonstrate her presence and her awareness of Jane being here tonight, so this was the most important thing (Jacob went quiet for a few seconds.) I think on this occasion it was the loving thought that was the most important thing. I think if there had been any other significance to the window you would have got it straight away.

Jacob then asked Carol:

> Did you feel anything straight away from looking in the window, or did it come afterwards?
> *It came afterwards. I initially got a feeling of warmth.*
> Yes, this is the warmth of the love coming through. I think she is giving Jane a beautiful loving warm feeling of comfort too, because it is a nice comforting scene which you portray, a safe scene, a homely scene, a scene of comfort and well being. I think this was the main point behind it.

So always try to go with your intuition, with what flows and comes straight away. Just be a little bit more cautious about what comes afterwards. It is not easy any of this (smiling.) If anyone says they find it easy, then I would question the messages they are giving you. Sometimes it may be easy but it is not easy all the time, and if people think it is going to be easy they may get too complacent. So do not worry about it not being easy, my friend.

Jane asked:

It's not always easy to interpret messages, but when you do and you feel the message within yourself, can you still be wrong?

Well it is true that sometimes you can be wrong. This is true. That is why it is most difficult, Jane, to be one-hundred-percent accurate all the time because there is always the possibility that you might get it wrong. Sometimes though, you will give something to someone, you will give them an interpretation which is your gut reaction, and then they will say something back to you and this may adjust your interpretation. You then know instantly that it feels right; it's a good fit. So perhaps your initial response wasn't quite right but when the person responds to you, you know instantly; ah that's what it means.

One night, in my other development group, I got a message for someone but the group leader also gave the person an interpretation based on what I'd received. I felt that her interpretation was wrong.

You must be careful, Jane, because when other people give you interpretations of what you have yourself received, they are no less subject to the difficulties of which I have spoken. In fact they might be quite wrong, because they are then approaching what *you* have been given from *their* perspective, and they will interpret it according to *their* perspective and this may be wrong.

Can this happen even with a leader who is more experienced?

Yes, you must still be cautious about this, even with someone more experienced, because they are not riding the same vibration as you. They are coming in **after** you have connected with the vibration, so they may not be picking the thing up in exactly the same way.

So you must be careful. I'm afraid, my friends, there are no easy solutions to this (smiling.) It is a matter of 'sucking it and see.' Do not let anyone portray this as an exact science, because it never will be an exact science like your physics is. It is more an art form, like painting a picture, and it's just like four people looking at the same picture and deciding what it was that the artist was trying to say. You will all come up with a different interpretation.

So there is something of this in the communication that we have to deal with from the spirit world. It is not an easy matter. And yet you can feel your way and sometimes you feel your way and feel instinctively right about it. Then sometimes somebody will give you something back by responding to you and you think; "Oh yes that's a good fit." But the important thing, my friends, even if the communications are not one-hundred-percent correct, is the act of linkage, of communion, which we value so much with you. We obviously wish to convey some messages, but my friends; you must appreciate the joy of communication as we make our endeavours in this enterprise from both sides.

Exercise:
Holding up hand

Jacob asked:

Go deep within your inner quietness please (couple of minutes pause.) I want you next to hold up one of your hands so that it is supported and you will not get tired. You can hold it close to your body or on a chair arm or whatever. I don't want you to get tired but I want you to hold up the most comfortable hand so that it is parallel with your body and it is upright. Now I want you to imagine that you are reaching out with the palm of your hand so that the palm of your hand is reaching out to the source of all, to the Great Self, to the Spiritual Essence of all things.

Now imagine your hand connecting with this Central Essence, this great Universal Self so that you have established a form of communication; you have formed a bond, a linkage, with this great Universal Energy. Now that you have formed this close bond with this energy I want you to imagine that you can now *receive* communication. And so, my friends, just wait; just wait to see what communication comes to you, in whatever form it comes. It may come in different forms to different people. (Few minutes pause.)

Following this exercise Jacob had this to say:

> I would suggest that you practise what you feel comfortable with and what you find helpful and dismiss the rest. This is fine because we each must find our own way, what works for us and what blends with our own energies and abilities.

Chapter 13

Jacob Session 6

Philosophy Night

Jacob began the session by informing us that this was going to be a philosophy night. He told us he would not give us any new exercises tonight and explained later that the point of the exercises, on this occasion, was that the Spirit Group were working with us to help us to discover some philosophy; both within ourselves and within the images we receive. In the 'feedback' below, Jacob demonstrates how a developing medium might go about interpreting their images and his response to Andrew's image offers us a good example of how images can be used to impart philosophy.

Jacob began:

This time we will just simply go within without any exercise other than bringing the mind to stillness, a still receptive point. So simply start to let your mind go quiet. I want you to get to a point where you have brought your mind to a still quiet point and then when you have achieved this for a few minutes we will see if any thoughts flash into your mind. While you are achieving this still quiet point if you feel thoughts coming to you then you must dismiss them, let them drop away without being too 'pushy' about it. If you are too 'pushy,' thoughts don't like that and they start to push back. You understand me? Once you have achieved your still quiet point and you are resting in a still receptive state then we shall see what comes.

So let us start to go quiet and make ourselves receptive to those energies that are around us but sit openly and not with any particular expectations in mind.

Jacob left us for a few minutes and then asked us for our feedback.

Feedback:

Jane

I saw a fence, folded arms, an eagle, and a pyramid made out of crystal. I thought the fence was an obstacle, the folded arms an authority figure and the eagle represented freedom and flight. The pyramid preserves things.

Jacob assisted by taking Jane's interpretation a little further:

We would suggest also that the pyramid has other associations of eternity, and it was made of crystal, we will associate this with *eternal wisdom*. We would concur with your interpretation. We would agree that, as you say, the fence represents an obstacle. Folded arms to us would represent *peace* but you may be right. We would say that the eagle does represent flight; it can also fly high above all obstacles. It can transcend all obstacles, for what is a fence to an eagle. It is nothing.

Therefore, we would say that you can overcome obstacles by and through the taking on of eternal wisdom which will enable you to fly free above all obstacles. So you must adopt a position of wisdom with all your daily dealings or tribulations. You can transcend all these things through eternal wisdom. But, **Eternal Wisdom**, although it sounds highfaluting, sombre, high-powered, and so on, **resides in daily life.**

Jacob then asked another member of the group to tell him what he'd seen. It's interesting to note with this feedback that, unlike the previous one, Jacob picked out just one image and told the person that this one was the most important one. For us it was further confirmation that we can sometimes get bogged down when we receive several images at once, and in this case it was only the first that had any significance.

Andrew

I saw a garden and a bowl of water, which reflected the clouds in the sky. There was a small fire, but it was in control, some circular stones, and a man who looked like a wizard looking at the fire.

The most important thing in all this is your bowl of water with the sky reflected in it. This symbolises Oneness of all things, the interpenetrating nature of this Oneness in all things. If you truly believe, if you truly know in your heart this Oneness, then you can sit beside your fire or anywhere else and feel an eternal peace. For the one who understands this truly has no need to move, to go anywhere, for all is with him as he sits in Oneness.

Andrew said he didn't fully understand. This was clearly to be a philosophy night because Jacob then went on to describe what he meant by the One Mind:

*   *   *

Well the nature of the whole world, the nature of reality is this sacred divine Oneness. The One Mind *is* the inner reality, the outer reality, the *only* reality. If you truly know the One Mind, if you are truly at One with Its nature—and straight away we get into trouble because we are talking about *It* as though *It* is an *It*, which would suggest that it is *apart* from us and it isn't,—but if we can truly understand that *Its* own nature is *our* nature, because it is inherently, implicitly, the nature of All Things. All things are with us at this instant in time, there is nothing that is without us.

How does the bowel of water symbolise this?

Because you have all things below in your bowl of water, all things above are reflected in it. It symbolises the Oneness of what is above and what is below, down here. It is only symbolic. We could give you other images as well that would mean the same thing.

Jacob referred to a guided meditation, Isleen, another member of the Spirit Group, had provided recently. He reminded us of the image we'd received, of just *one* candle in a cave with mirrors all around and the one candle reflecting in all of them. He went on:

We are like the reflections of the 'one candle,' my friends, but even our reflection is reflected in the reflection of our friend, our brother, and our sister. So there is Oneness in all this. We cannot approach this easily with our minds, yet we can know it with our hearts, our inner hearts. There is Oneness in all life, One Lifeblood flowing through all of us, One Eternal Reality flowing through all of us, changeless, timeless. And if we really know this, if we really experience this, we have divine peace, for there is nothing that we are without. We are At One, in harmony with all, the inner nature of all. So I would say your bowl of water, Andrew, is a symbol of Oneness.

Andrew wanted further explanation about his image and asked:

What did the fire with stones around it, making it safe, mean?

We think that your fire is too safe, my friend. We think you need to take away the stones, the nice safe round stones that surround it. Perhaps you need to scatter the boulders that protect this fire of yours. You need to let the fire catch, spread the fire. We think you need to reveal more of yourself, to show more of yourself to the world and the people you encounter, to let the flames catch them.

Jacob explained that they had given Paul (the medium) a chess piece of the Bishop. He asked us what the Bishop represents to us. We told him it could only be moved diagonally. Jacob explained the purpose of Paul's image:

We often do only move in one way in life. We get stuck with our movements like the bishop who can only move diagonally to it. It is like a parable of our lives also. The purpose of this image is that we often get stuck in our way of responding to things, to situations and to people, so it's almost like someone comes along and says, you can only move one way or another. It is like we programme ourselves or we let other people programme us, so we get stuck in a rut. We then wind ourselves up in a certain way and off we go very predictably and we get more and more stuck.

Another way of thinking about this is that we take on a role and we stick ourselves in that role and yet, my friends, inside here (pressing his heart area) we are so creative, we are capable of so many different ways of responding, capable of so many different ways of thinking about things and doing things, but we get stuck. We get stuck my friends, and it is not healthy, it is not creative, it is a great pity.

You talked before about problems in the world (referring to Hai's previous talk on war) and I say to you that many problems of the world are that people are 'knight people,' 'bishop people,' 'pawn people,' and so on, and this is helpful to those who would manipulate you, because they know how you will move. People need to look at you in a different way, think about you in a different way; this will not do them any harm because they have to sit up and think. And, because of that it will make *them* think in a different way which will help them also. So it is always right to think symbolically, but you need to think in different ways about possibilities here.

It was at this point that Jacob explained to us the purpose of the first couple of exercises that night (as described at the beginning of this chapter.) He then went on to try something else; however, the philosophy theme continued.

Group exercise:
Interpreting Symbols/Communication

The technique used in the exercise below is used in many development circles. The idea is that each group member takes it in turn to quietly go within while the rest of the group send out loving thoughts to that person. The purpose is that the person meditating will enhance their own 'receiving' abilities because of the increased energy sent from the other group members.

Jacob asked the group to send loving thoughts to Eileen while she went into her silence. He explained what he wanted her to do and said:

> Try thinking about a pond, a pond which at first its waters are ruffled. You can see the ripples and the waves but slowly and surely they start to settle down and you imagine the pond going calm and stiller until you have a millpond. It has a smooth surface—like if you could polish it—it's so still. When you have got that then just let go of it and see what comes. Don't work at it just see what comes. (Few minutes pause then Eileen gave feedback)

Eileen's feedback

I saw a church with a tall steeple and it was in the centre of a pine forest.

Jacob wanted more detail and asked:
   What was the pine forest like was it flat?
   It was flat and it was a deep thick green.
   And so the church was enclosed in the forest?
   Yes, as though the forest was protecting it in some way.
   A dilemma here but go on. You go inside?
   There was a tiled floor with a pattern on it. There were no chairs and because the floor looked so cold I wondered where the people could sit. I then saw cubicles around the side of the church. It was a church for every religion.

Jacob asked Eileen what 'feelings' she had about it. She replied:
   I thought it was something to do with me wanting a place for people to go, to achieve peace.

Jacob did not immediately respond to Eileen's answer but instead said:

   We want you to try this experiment: Just go quiet again. Go within yourself and imagine yourself in this church again and once you are there we want you to cast your eyes down to the tiled floor and see if you see anything.

Eileen answered after a few minutes pause.
   I couldn't see a pattern but I thought it was mother of pearl and inlaid with different colours, though mostly white or off white and small coloured pieces.

Jacob responded:
   Mother of pearl; Pearl of wisdom. Is this not remarkable my friends? We go from nothing to this.

Jacob was about to demonstrate how, with a little patience, much more could be discovered from an image than was originally thought possible. However, before doing this he asked the rest of the group for their interpretations on Eileen's image. One group member ventured:

She has a desire to nurture everyone, to bring everyone together in peace and harmony.

Jacob replied:

Yes it is certainly to do with inner sanctuary; sanctuary in the heart of the forest. But this is a haven, a sanctuary of peace. It is not so much that the forest is hiding the church or protecting the church from the world but rather it is like; we may go to a favourite spot where we will have peace. There is something special about the church. Good, rich treasure, and you are puzzled, Eileen, because you find no seats. You then realise that there are cubicles; 'sanctuary within a sanctuary' but this symbolises the sanctuary within, the church within, the temple within.

There is a rich temple, a golden temple, within all of us, a temple of wisdom and peace. So you provide this facility where people can come together to go within. We truly may come together to go within and in going within we are connecting with each other and we are connecting to wisdom; *pearl of wisdom*. So having come together to go within, to partake of the One Wisdom, One Peace, One Heart, we come out of our cubicles. We bow to each other (laughs) in recognition of what we each have discovered and what we know each of us has discovered, then we walk out to the open and we walk out along the paths of the pine forest, into the world, and take out our love and wisdom.

Jacob then described the symbol the Spirit Group had given, Paul the medium, while in trance. He told us:

We give him just one solitary pine tree on a hill. Because when you all go out through the pine forest (symbolically) it is as if you become one solitary pine tree on a hill, *that everyone may see*, like a lighthouse to help people find their way.

Group exercise:
Continuation of above plus 'Train reaction' exercise

In this exercise Jacob gives us detailed instructions to help us interpret our messages. He demonstrates how by using a 'train reaction' method you can receive and interpret a whole message from spirit. Jacob began:

> We will now try an experiment that uses a 'train reaction' to receive messages. So go quietly within. I want you to think with loving thoughts of the person on your right and wait to see if an image forms. (Few minutes pause then feedback)

Feedback:

Eileen told Andrew:

> *I saw a very small sailing ship in a harbour. The ship was then taken away and I could only look at the sea. Also saw a white seagull.*

Jacob began to instruct Eileen how to interpret her message. He told her:

> *Blend* the sea with the seagull. (Notice the emphasis on *blend* and how Jacob ignores the boat, because it has disappeared)

After listening to Eileen's attempts to do this Jacob helped by explaining:

> The seagull was free—tremendous space, freedom, expansiveness, and a free spirit. And with freedom and expansiveness comes all the possibilities of it.

Eileen commented:
> *The harbour seemed cluttered.*
> What is the fundamental thing about harbours? Harbours are often about work, busy, everyday world activity. *So we've got to put all this together.* (Again the emphasis on the *blending*)

Jacob spoke directly to Andrew whom the message was meant for.

> Sometimes you want your mind to be equilibrium perhaps; sometimes you want your mind to be looking on a vast sea of contemplations, freedom, expansiveness, or creativity. You cannot be

there all the time but you would like to bring some of that into work, to have a peaceful equilibrium mind in work.

Andrew's feedback for Jane

Andrew told Jacob:

I got four images. They started with a picture of Jane and this led to the colour of her hair. I then got a bird, a pelican flying high in the sky. I saw an image of Jane as a child playing, catching fish in a pond on a summer's day. She was very happy. I also saw the sun and moon coming together in an eclipse and some curtains closing.

Jacob asked for clarification:
So you saw a bird first, then Jane fishing, then an eclipse. What do you make of this, Andrew?
Well the pelican is a community bird and they work together. I thought this was a link to family closeness in that her family gives her strength. The image I got of Jane fishing I felt was a happy childhood memory link and I thought the eclipse was Jane's spirituality coming together into an eclipse. The curtains were Victorian and were being closed. They were very warm curtains and decorative. I'm not sure what that meant.

Yes we would say also with this eclipse, Jane that perhaps you should not think in terms of this and that, opposites. It is not a case of doing things this way or that way. There may be a hundred other ways of doing them.

With regard to the curtains, we see this almost as curtains on a stage, like as if these curtains symbolise curtains closing on stage at the end of a play—like the end of one thing and the start of another. We see this as the start of greater freedom for you because the curtains were Victorian. This represents a past age, the past symbolises the finish of one era then the start of another. It is moving on, moving on from the past. It is not like—cut the past—but moving on from the past with greater freedom, greater unfoldment, evolvement, and growth. The Victorian room seems stuffy and so the closing of the curtains indicates growth, a closing of the curtains and a moving on.

The pelican remember, has a big beak but also a big crop, and can store a lot of food—resources. So you can store resources to use later—strength and wisdom, to use later. That is a good sign.

Some people try to build a foundation for themselves but the foundation is not strong enough, so when they meet their first obstacle they go under. However, you have the ability to build strong foundations for yourself. You can take on board advice from people, your own inner reflections, inner wisdom, wisdom and guidance you receive from others, and so on, and turn it into a strong foundation which can see you through difficult times of life. So you are a good master of your own resources.

Jane told Eileen

I saw an old fashioned pram but no baby. I thought it was the birth of something new. I felt positive emotions with you; it was lovely. I also saw a celebration cake with candles, a bottle of champagne and people with you. It was a lovely feeling. Then I was in the Middle Ages. There was an archer firing arrows but not in aggression. It was the arrow of truth. Throughout all of this the emotions were lovely, happy, peace and joy, very positive.

Jacob responded:

Well you know you are near the mark, Jane, for you generally have a baby in a pram and while we have a baby in the pram we nurture it, mollycoddle it.

Jacob turned to Eileen:

You are doing this with your book, Eileen. But before long it will become a toddler and it will walk off. (Eileen was still in the process of putting together our first book when she received this message and Jacob was referring to this)

I think that the arrow also refers to the book. You focused on it and it brought results straight in your direction. Your focus produced a straight target and will bring much joy. You will get letters thanking you for the book.

*   *   *

Jacob closed the session with these words:

We wish you great peace, great happiness, and great insight—and (smiling) great chess players.

Chapter 14

Jacob Session 7

Faith & Hope
Practise, Practise, and more Practise

The following is a short extract from our seventh session with Jacob. Just prior to this communication we'd received our third visit from a spirit who said she was Queen Elizabeth the 1st. When Jacob eventually came through he referred to the 'waiting station' and said he'd been waiting for Elizabeth to finish. He laughed and said he had to wait for *Royalty* to finish before coming through and added:

"She is a very nice lady to talk to and does not have all those airs and graces now."

Jacob has always emphasised the importance of practise between sessions and started by asking if we'd managed to practise since our last meeting. Eileen said although she'd been practising she didn't think she'd accomplished much. Jacob replied:

Well you should just keep going you know, just keep trying, and you will find that before too long you will have accomplished something. It is like the lady you've just spoken to (referring to our previous spirit visitor) who told you, you must have faith, you must carry on, like a boulder going downhill, and eventually you will get to the bottom of the valley.

Traditionally it is believed that developing mediumship is easier when in a group because the combined energies of the group help with spirit connection. One member asked Jacob:

Do the combined energies in the group, make it easier than practising alone?
It is easier because you accomplish more. Because you are working with each other, the energies all come together and you support each other. It is more the matter of support for each other, which is beneficial to you. You must be hopeful in your endeavours. Without hope we are nothing, we get nowhere, but if we have hope we may indeed reach the stars.

Jacob asked what exercises we'd found useful. One group member said she had found that visualising the seashore in the moonlight had been helpful, as was a particular exercise about 'feeling.' The exercise had really got to her centre and she had connected with the source of pure love. Jacob told her:

It is like this 'knitting' you talk of, Jane, (when she goes deep, Jane often gets an image of intersecting lines of energy which she often refers to as 'knitting') because you are trying to reach to the other world, our world. It is rather like—there are lots of strands of wool but they are very ephemeral and nebulous. You are simply trying to gather them up in the best way you can with your reaching out with your mind, heart, feeling, and sensitivity. So you can gather all these things, all these strands of wool, to make something of them. I know it's not easy but it is a matter of continuing perseverance.
It's difficult, Jacob, finding a time to meditate when I am also calm.
Yes you are quite right. You must try to find some peace in your day so you are not hurried, your mind is not hurried, is at peace, and content. (Smiling) Then you can give it some freedom to gather in the wool.

Exercise:
Interpreting Symbols

Jacob began the session by saying:

> I think we will just simply go within on this occasion. So I would ask you all to just float within yourselves quietly, calmly, until you find your centre and your inner depths. I would like you to stay there for a few minutes to see what may come.
>
> So just let your mind go into its centre, to its inner stillness, its calmness, its quietness: Just stay within, simply contemplate. Let things come, let things happen naturally. (There was a few minutes pause, then Jacob brought us back and asked for feedback.)

Feedback:

Jane

> *I saw a twister (hurricane) a basket, a big daisy, and a safety pin.*
> What did you think about this?
> *I'm not sure. Can you help me out please, Jacob?*

The daisy was about staying full of hopefulness for it's a bright flower of hope of joy. The basket was empty inside and could mean that you have no axe to grind, no wish to achieve anything for yourself. We feel this safety pin you got is a security thing with you because we carry safety pins around with us 'just in case'. This is a 'just in case' safety pin, and you may not need it.

Andrew

> *I saw the countryside, a deep crater, and a small pool. The water was dense and heavy. There was a yellow leaf floating around. It was peaceful. To me it represents my inner self, peaceful. I'm not sure about the yellow leaf though.*

Yellow is joy, it is love, it is wisdom, and it is energy. So I think this is about recognising the beauty within, the inner beauty of us all. There is a yellow flower at the centre of us all of great beauty, of great tranquillity and great depth.

Chapter 15

Jacob Session 8

In an earlier chapter Jacob explained how we should go about contacting our guide. One night a new member joined the development group and asked Jacob a similar question. We decided to print the communication here because it covers others aspects of communication which are not covered in the earlier session.

Exercise:

Jacob led us into the following exercise.

We will try and connect with our guides so I will give you some idea of what I would like you to try. This is a very simple exercise but it can have many benefits.

We need to go quietly, calmly within, and then I will ask you to reach out to your guide, reach out to that benevolent spiritual influence, and ask them to influence you in some way. I then simply want you to become aware of everything you sense. This may be a presence perhaps or you may receive a message. Just take note of everything that you become aware of.

Feedback

Jane described seeing a vision with words. Jacob asked her:

So the words came with the vision. You did not hear them but they came with the vision?

Yes.

So you are connected to your guide primarily through inner vision, but sometimes this inner vision can also bring words that we do not 'hear,' but 'sense' in some strange way. It is like the words come from within. It is primarily a way of connecting with spirit, which is visual.

Len described a similar sensation but also received a vibration of 'feeling.' Jacob responded:

As I said before there is often one means of communication that is particularly strong in us but there may be another means of communication, which is present, but is not well developed and is weaker than the other. However, if we start to become aware of it we can, sort of, give it a boost. (Smiling) We would not encourage you to boost it too much, at the expense of your primary one, until your primary one is well developed, but it is helpful, nevertheless, to become aware of the secondary means of communication, which is available to you. So it is useful that you recognise it. You then give it the opportunity to gradually develop alongside the other senses.

Carol told Jacob:

I got a vibration from behind and a shiver across my neck. I saw colours and had a sensation of light-headedness and lifting up. I also received a name.
This is more sensory, more at a 'feeling' level. Some people find this communication harder to relate to it because it feels more nebulous, more difficult to get a hold of; nevertheless, it is not to be disparaged because of this.

Carol replied:
Yes it is more difficult. I feel I argue with myself because I'm not sure I'm making it up.
Yes it is more indistinct in some way, and therefore, it causes our mind more problems in trying to link with it and apprehend it. But it is important that we recognise that it is yet another form of communication with the spirit world. Therefore, it is simply a matter of gently going with it. We must just try to connect with it, patiently and gradually, and we will get more communication and a stronger sense of what the communication is about.

The colours you received are, sort of, in between because they are partly visual but quite strongly sensory as well. So you must approach these colours by asking yourself what you *feel* about them, but you need to, *feel* the question, more in the *heart* than in the mind. Do you follow me? It's more about an inner gut reaction to how you *feel* about these colours. Our guides will be able to 'walk on the road,' which is built by these means, and they may well use other means of communication in future.

Jacob went on to ask Carol what she felt about her colours. She answered:

They were calming. They started green and moved to a stronger purple as I connected more.

Yes this is partly symbolic. The green symbolising the physical world and vibration, shifting through to purple, which symbolises a high spiritual vibration. So in part they are using the colours in this way to symbolise the shift. So as you get the purple you must be open and receptive. (Note: the purple, *in this case*, was the stronger colour. With someone else another colour may be the stronger one.)

Jacob turned to Ann and asked what she'd received during the exercise. Ann replied:

I felt my guide approach from behind and put an arm around me.
Which way does the arm come round you?
Not sure.
Is it an arm with a left or right hand?
Left hand.
Ah then it comes around your left arm. You see the clues we can pick up. We will use this as an example if you don't mind.

We have to think in this way because it often happens that we feel that we are getting communication but we cannot make 'head nor tail' of it. So by asking ourselves—what did we sense about this; was it a right or left hand I could see, or feel? And it can sometimes take us a bit further along the road.

Jacob turned to Ann again and asked:
Could you see your guide, when you looked?

Yes.
So how does he look?

Ann described her guide and the message she'd received. Jacob responded:

So he gives you a twofold message and you have connected well. It is mainly visual but also sensory what you have experienced here. Did you get words with the vision?
The words came with the vision but not in an audible way.
Yes. Sometimes it is because our minds are interpreting the vision. Sometimes there are words that they truly are trying to slip in. It is like your computers. I understand it is possible for you to make an image that you can transfer to another computer and within that image it can contain other information. Is that so? So it is like that with us. It is like we convey to you an image, a vision, but it is like there is a code written within it and the words come through the code. So primarily you get the vision but the code gives you that little bit extra (smiling) added value. I have help with that analogy (referring to other spirits.) You see we all have helpers. There are helpers all around me slipping in the odd word here and there.

We can all practise connecting with our guides and giving them the benefit of communicating with us, and so you must see it in that way too. It is not like you become a sponge graciously awaiting the flow of the divine waters. (laughing) It is not like that for you do us a kindness by allowing us to communicate with you. Both benefit; your guide will benefit, for you provide an opportunity for him or her to help you, and *you* benefit, hopefully, from the influence of wisdom they offer at the time. But it is partnership my friends, partnership. You must not look upon your guides as 'holy ones;' it is not helpful. They wish to help you and you can help them by allowing them to help you.

Another member of the group asked:

*But—**could** they be holy, Jacob?*

Jacob smiles and answers:

Yes they could be holy, my dear Jane. They could be holy but what does it matter? If they are trying to influence you, help you in a beneficial way, this is what it is all about so the label of holy does not matter. We are all holy, as Hai has indicated before. We are all holy.

If we have more than one guide, would we see every guide in the same way or do they all have their own way of making contact.

They sometimes have different ways of making contact so it is important never to be fixed. You must not turn anything into a rigid pattern. You must utilise your brain's capacity, one-hundred-percent (laughs.) You must not put yourself in a straightjacket.

Now if you know who your main guide is when you connect, you automatically assume that it will be this guide who comes to you, so if you don't receive the usual 'sense' that your main guide is present, you start wondering where he or she is. There is no big problem with this but our expectations can limit us. It might be, on a particular occasion that another guide may wish to connect, and this guide may approach from a different direction or will convey a different feel. When Hai and Isleen come through Paul he is aware of a different *feel*, different energy vibration. It is like *experiencing* a temperament but instead of 'seeing' it in front of you, you become aware of it *inside* you. At this level it is more a *feeling* vibration and you can in time become accustomed to this and work out the difference.

Can two people experience the same guide at the same time?

It is possible. It is possible that a guide can connect with two people at once. Yes it is possible.

Chapter 16

Excerpts from Jacob's Workshops

Shortly after the sessions in the previous chapters, Jacob told us that we'd now got sufficient material for our book. Nevertheless, we continued to record all our sessions, which later developed more into workshops, and at times Jacob would make a point of asking us to include something else that came up which had not previously been covered. Below you will find, not only the additional things that he asked us to include, but also some of the friendly chats that we continue to have with Jacob and which we thought might be of interest as well.

Out of Body Travel

We quickly realised that Jacob seemed to like nothing better than to chat to us about any matter that occurred to us, or him. In the communication below he is asked about 'out of body travel.'

Recently when meditating I found myself drifting away. It was a sensation of being there but something within me was trying to drift onto the side.
  Good, this is very good. This may be perhaps something like the start of 'out of body travel,' or it may just be that you are becoming aware of your spirit, and your spirit is drifting slightly out of your body. It may not go anywhere but you *are* its energies so you are aware of them. It may also be that you can develop this to become an 'out of body traveller' and (smiling) visit the stars. So it may be, that you can develop this travelling ability, to look at and explore different places.

I thought only very wise and experienced people could do that.

No, it can happen quite by chance. It does not happen too often by will, not at first, you understand. It happens more by chance or you sometimes get a feel for it, like when you first learn to ride a bike. You do not know exactly how you ride a bike, do you, but your body gets a *feel* for it; you get your sense of balance and you are away, and it is a bit like this sometimes with this out of body travel. So you just get a feel for it, know something is happening, and you assist it. You put yourself in the right frame of mind for your spirit to actually disengage from the body, perhaps briefly at first, and it might go to the ceiling, or move along the side of the body. You may then find that you can develop this skill, and will therefore, drift more easily into this state, which will enable you to travel around. As time goes on you may find that you develop a knack, an ability to know how to go about it, to more consciously bring it about. Therefore, if you have the right state of mind, the right conditions around you, you can do it readily whenever you choose. You could explore this my friend, no harm could come to you in this. You just reach out positively to nice places to travel.

Someone else commented:

One time I felt that my body was about a foot above me and it felt like it had stretched, but when I opened my eyes I was still on the bed.

Some people practise out of body travel this way because it may put their minds, so to speak, in a different part of the room. They may *project* their mind. At first this is only an imagining, a mental projection. But if they practise and place their mind in another part of the room they could well find their mind has moved to that part of the room. With time, the right frame of mind, patience, and lack of anxiety—you could do this. But if there is anxiety in this practice it is self-defeating. There is no quicker way to snap back into your body than if you get a bit anxious and afraid of what is going on. But there is no harm in this if you approach it in the right way. So you may try to practise this but you need to do this consistently to get into the right frame of mind, the right approach to it. If you try it for one month and leave it for six months it is not going to work; patience and regular practise is required.

Can you offer advice on the length of time we should practise and how often?

Well you could practise daily for a short time say fifteen minutes each day and this is better that wearing yourself out. Some people wear themselves out with too much practise and then they just tie themselves in knots because they get wound up and anxious because they do not feel they are progressing. But the reason they do not progress is because they put too much **will** in their effort, whereas the essence of what we are trying to do in any of this development is to **let go**. When we are able to let go we have the greatest progress. Many people think; "Oh it is not happening so I must be doing something wrong, or not doing enough of it," etc, and while their mind is going around in these ever decreasing circles they undermine their potential, their ability to actually perceive things and to develop. It is **openness**, which is the most critical factor and requirement in all this.

So we would say—that it is best to practise for fifteen to twenty minutes at any one time. You will find that the first time you practise you may only achieve the desired state for a couple of minutes, but as you practise each day, you will find that as you start to reach for that state of mind that you are aspiring to, and you will go into it much quicker because you have practised. Therefore, once you are well practised you remain in that state for a greater time. So patience is the key, my friend, patience, and lack of anxiety.

Someone else asked a follow on question and Jacob responded by explaining some of the technicalities of communication through meditation:

If you develop generally, through meditation, would these other things develop as well?

Well it depends upon the kind of meditation of which you speak. You see—it is easy for us to 'ride' in upon an imaginative meditation for it awakens the faculty of your imaginative mind and we can then, (smiling) like a glove puppet, put our hand into your pocket and move it around. We can make use of the images that you are creating in your mind; we can tap into them, shape them, manipulate, and use them—with the best of intentions you understand.

Also if you are able to create some spaces in your meditation, it gives us some gaps to move around to try to attempt communication. If your mind is cluttered with mental thoughts and agitation it is so difficult for us to intervene in that. It can, in certain situations, certain times of need, still be accomplished when some intervention on our part is desirable. It is most difficult for us in this situation though and is not something we can readily achieve.

The rules, the principles are so simple. We have tried out with you various exercises, ways of opening up to communication, but they are all much of a much-ness and are all very simple in their essence. It is just that sometimes people connect with one way much more readily than another, for you are all human beings. You are all varied in your tastes, your mental equipment and in your approaches, and sometimes people find one approach easier than another.

Some people gaze into water for instance and they find this helps them to get images. Others gaze at the moon and get something. Others simply sit and reach out to us and they will get something. So it varies, and it is as well to practise with various methods to see what works for you, but without becoming a 'stamp collector.' You understand me? I do not know the right term. So we must experiment but we must not do so unduly. We must find the right path for each of us, stick with it for a while, and then test it out.

But each time we communicate with each other you learn a bit more. I learn a bit more too, because I learn how to express some of these ideas and I get feedback from you in your responses, which is valuable. So we have got to try things out in openness and in a mind of experiment.

*   *   *

Another night Jacob had given us the usual meditation and asked us to wait for something to form out of the mist. He then turned to Eileen for feedback. Eileen told him her pink mist had changed to blue but added that she found it difficult because she was too busy asking questions. Jacob replied:

Well I can understand why you do that but it is not always the best way. Sometimes, when you see something like that, it is best to just *silently* question. It is like your mind *becomes* a question mark so you are not actually forming words to form the question, your mind just *becomes* the question. *This is quite important Eileen, and you should put it in the book please,* because this often happens. People ask lots of questions. This can work sometimes, but often it can be difficult because when people start to ask lots of questions in their mind, they are thinking; "what should I ask," and this can break the connection because their minds become too busy again.

So it is best to simply turn your *whole mind* into the question. It does not matter what the question is—there is no question in fact—because you see, the 'trick' is that the spirit knows what answer it wants to give you, so you don't need to know the question because they've already got the answer. You follow me? So all you've got to do is *be* one big question, and they connect with your question and give you the answer.

Feeling & Intuition

Jacob asked if we'd been practising and one member commented that she seemed to have stopped getting anything. Jacob told her:

> I am sure you are getting something. Sometimes you do not realise how much you are getting. You need a sort of 'penny pot.' You put a penny in each time you get something so you realise how much you get.

Jacob turned to another member of the group and asked:

> Have you seen anything since our last meeting, John?
> *No, sorry, Jacob, I haven't been meditating.*
> Well you do not need to meditate so much all the time. You can sometimes just get a glimmer of something that will flash before your eyes. When this happens it is useful to see if you get any *feeling* with it, *intuition* about it. But do not ask a question; "what do I feel," instead, just *feel*, because if you ask; "what do I feel," then you put a separation between yourself and what you see. So you have to, sort of—reach out and *feel*, without asking the question in words. I hope you follow me?

Yes but it's hard to do that.

Yes, but you, sort of—connect with your *feelings*, your *intuition*. It is hard to explain, but perhaps you have some sense of what I mean. It is like when you connect with us generally you see. The feeling, the emotion, is very important for us on our vibration, and if you are to connect with us it is useful not to connect at the level of thought, but of *feeling*; to reach out to us with your *emotions*, your *feeling*, your *intuition*, for this is the vibration where you can most easily reach us; the vibration of *feeling*. So if you reach out with feelings of love to us, it assuredly connects with us and we with you, and it establishes a good bond and connection with us that we may communicate with each other. So *feeling* is very important.

But again you see, it is just merely reaching out with feeling, reaching out with love, with emotion, with affection, and this achieves the connection. It is like you caress someone. If you caress someone it establishes communication in an indistinct subtle but powerful way.

Picking up Sensations & Physical Conditions from Spirits

Someone commented that she'd got a sharp pain when she'd contacted spirit. Jacob commented:

You must distance yourself if you need to. As you become more sensitive to spirits, especially if you are sensitive to someone near the earth plane, they may affect you by giving you physical sensations. They do not mean any harm by this, but they are trying to connect with you, and they may give you a sense of a condition that they experienced while last on the earth plane. Therefore, you need to discriminate between this feeling that they are giving you, and your own bodily sensations. It is like they drop an emotion, a sensation into you, and therefore, you must be careful to recognise this and say silently to yourself; "there is nothing in this of me. There is nothing in this, which is particular to my body at this time. It is someone else who has experienced this and they are trying to connect and share with me an experience that they had." So in other words, you put some emotional distance between it and yourself. So just acknowledge it and try to withdraw from it. Accept the understanding, the connection, but then withdraw from it so you do not experience any further discomfort.

Auras

A visitor asked about colours he sometimes sees in a person's aura. He told Jacob he'd seen orange once and later discovered that the person had been angry with someone. He asked Jacob if, in that instance, the colour orange had related to the person being annoyed. Jacob replied:

Possibly, but you see, sometimes what might be happening is that you are connecting with *one* aspect of it. So Orange can be about, as you say, vexation perhaps, but it can also be about energy attached to the person at that time. So someone might connect with the orange and feel that the person has excess energy that can be used to advantage, whilst another person may connect with the feeling that it is something to do with vexation. However, there will be an element of truth in both, for when we are vexed we often have surplus energy. So we have to feel our way with this.

Difficulty in Connecting with a Guide

One of our Home Circle members said she was not always able to connect with her guide. This question has been asked many times; however, Jacob patiently responded:

You mustn't worry about this, my dear, Jane. You must just reach out to him with your love and compassion, and await influence and development. Sometimes we connect with you in subtle ways, sometimes in more obvious ways. The trouble is, that it is human nature, that when we are able to connect with you in *one* of the more obvious ways, you take this as *the* way; therefore, when it doesn't happen again in quite the same way, you think something is going wrong and you are not connecting. So we must not have too many preconceptions.

It is like what Hai was talking to you about before; it is like being *non-attached* in the manner and quality of our connection but trusting in it nevertheless. And we can connect and we will be able to influence you in ways we hope will be helpful. Sometimes this can be in an unexpected way though, like an influence that comes into your life or a perception of what you see about you. It can happen in a subtle way.

I suppose I want it to be like a two-way conversation with someone who is actually here.

No, this is not often possible but it doesn't mean that it is not real because of that. We have to allow for the subtlety of communication between the worlds.

Someone else asked:

So would Jane know whether she'd made a connection with her guide?

This question, in various forms, had also been asked before. And again, with love and patience, Jacob responded:

We have told you before, my friend, that if you reach out to us it is not a matter of whether the connection *can* be established; the connection will assuredly be established—like a lightening flash, so you should not doubt the connection. The manner of our communication may vary from time to time but the connection is assured. There are not the problems that you have with your telephones.

Is that why when we sometimes ask a question and feel we've not had an answer, we can then read something and find that the material contains the answer?

Yes, because we use your sensitivity—your mind is already preoccupied perhaps, with some issue, and we are able to use your experience of reading a book, or something like that, in order to convey some kind of answer to you.

*   *   *

Jacob always seems able to intuitively pick up when someone is experiencing a problem. If they don't volunteer it he will simply turn his attention to them and ask them a question. This happened immediately after he'd finished answering the question above. Jacob suddenly turned to one of our younger members of the group and asked:

Are you aware of your guide, Paul?
No I don't seem to have the patience. I just get frustrated and angry and put it off until the next day.

Yes, but you say you do not have the patience so you must first get your mind into a calm state of meditation. You could imagine you are quietly meditating beside a lake. (Jacob stopped to ask if Paul was ok with water before continuing) You could imagine yourself sat on a rock overlooking a lake, so, in other words, you can sit on a big rock sticking out onto a lake and you are high above the water and have the opportunity to look down into the lake. Now—you must go into a calm state of meditation and absorb yourself into the scene of the lake, perhaps the forest on the far side or the beautiful sky above. Look at nothing in particular but just *absorb* yourself in the beautiful scene. When your mind is calm and (smiling) you've tricked it into letting go of your frustration and anger, simply look down into the water and see what you see.

Jacob told us he would help Paul by giving us a meditation to help demonstrate his point. He said:

We shall call this, The Paul's Rock Meditation. This will be a famous meditation inspired by you. The Paul's Rock Meditation will become famous throughout the world, (smiles) perhaps not to many people in the world—but famous throughout the world.

Paul's Rock Meditation

Jacob continued:

Please go within and close your eyes. You can see a beautiful swirling mist of whatever colour you wish. As you look through this mist visualise a landscape forming on the other side. The mist clears and you can see the beautiful hills and mountains in the distance and greenery all around.

Start to step through the mist and you will notice that the scenery becomes more clear, more beautiful, and vibrant. You find yourself in a landscape of hills and forests with mountains in the distance. A short distance away you can see a beautiful lake so you find a path that you may walk along to reach it. You start along the path walking carefully and gently along.

In the distance you can see a little deer. It seems quite content and happy just eating the grass, watching you from time to time, content and at his ease. You pass him and give him a little stroke upon his head. Now carry on along the path towards the lake, and in a short time you find yourself approaching the lakeside.

As you look ahead you can see a great flat rock that juts out into the waters of the lake. Now, I want you to walk slowly and gently onto this rock and sit safely on its edge. Look over into the beautiful clear lake. As you look over into its pure waters you can see the reflection of your face on the surface. Stare at your reflection, gaze at it, peacefully, contentedly. And as you continue to stare at your reflection, you may find that another reflection may start to appear, which is to your interest and benefit.

Following the meditation Paul asked:

When we do these exercises do we stop when we get one image or should we carry on receiving them until you call us back?

Sometimes it is worth focussing on one because when you get one image and you focus upon it you get more in its wake, you get more detail or you get another aspect explained to you about your first image. So sometimes it is like as if you set your telescope upon it and it helps you connect with other things to do with it. This can be useful.

*   *   *

Jacob told us that the following transcript would be useful for this book. The communication, and resulting feedback, took place following one of Jacob's exercises when he was helping us to contact our guide. We've included a short extract here. The communication gives the reader a flavour of the good natured humour which we've all come to associate with Jacob, as he shows that developing mediumship should be fun and is nothing to worry about or get too serious over. We have printed the extract, virtually as it was said.

Jacob's Message:
Contact with Spirit should be Fun

Jacob started by asking us all to go within and try to connect with our guide. After a few minutes he asked one member of the group, Susan, what, if anything, she'd received.

Susan replied:
I didn't get much except a flash of yellow. And then it seemed like a grey shadow as though someone was beside me shuffling around in my peripheral vision.

Jacob replied with humour:
Ah, a 'shuffling guide,' (Laughs) anything else?
No.

Jacob continued to smile:
So you say you got nothing, but you got a lot. You got energy with this yellow colour. So this guide brings you energy, (smiling again) this shuffling guide. So they bring you energy, much energy; they connect with you and the connection will be a good connection. They are new to you, I think, but they bring you much energy and you can connect with this energy to your benefit. You will become more aware of them as you focus upon them. You must have no fear about this. You feel o.k. about them?
Yes.
Good, (smiling again) you must just say; "Hello, it is you shuffling guide, how are you today."
Will they always come to me that way?
Yes, it may well be, yes.

Note: Jacob, when referring to guides, often uses the plural, i.e. they or them.

Jacob then went on to say:

With your permission we will ask Eileen to put this in our 'shopping guide' (this book) for it will help some people. Some people are nervous of guides or spirits you see, so part of our mission here is to alleviate or reduce any fears or apprehensions. For if you reach out with good intent you will only benefit from good intent. Like attracts like is an eternal principle. So no one must have any fear or apprehension if they reach out with good intent, with compassionate love, for they will receive compassionate love in return. So, (smiling) by referring to *shuffling guide*, it helps to diminish the fears and anxiety of some folk, so it is useful and helpful to them. I think this will be good for our next book, so with your permission, Susan, we will instruct Eileen, (laughs) ask her politely, to include it in the book.

* * *

New Session:

From time to time, we all receive images that we are unable to understand and which might seem a little daunting to us. The person who received the following image was concerned that it might be some kind of omen. However, when Jacob explained the meaning of the image, it all became clear.

There is no need to be disturbed by Images

After taking us through our exercise, Jacob asked for feedback. One member commented:

I got a lake. At first it was clear and beautiful. Then it became black, and full of oil. I saw a goldfish lying on top of it.

This communication could have come from a particular spirit person. However, you didn't see anyone; therefore, it could be that the spirit is expressing a *concern* that they wish you to be aware of and to reflect upon. It is a *general* concern.

You see, the scene is natural and beautiful but you see a lake of oil and a golden fish struggling for life in the oil. This is expressing a concern to you, a concern for the natural environment. For the natural environment should be as you first imagined the lake, in all its beauty and clarity, in health and purity, but humankind is polluting your earth, is strangling your earth with oil and pollution. And the good life of this earth is struggling because of this pollution, and you have lost many birds and fish because of it. So this is someone who wants to connect with you because of their concern for the natural world. They sense an affinity that you too are concerned and wish to share that with you. You may become more aware of the person as time goes on.

So the important thing about this is that—**you should not become disturbed by the images.** It may be clumsy on our part, to create a lake of oil (smiling) out of beautiful clear water, but if you do not become disturbed by the image you may find the message in it. The goldfish is symbolic of the sanctity of life and the rich potential of life. Life will triumph. Life will triumph in this goldfish. So there is a message of hope amidst this black oil.

Lateral Thinking & Flexibility

In the following transcript Jacob explains, when interpreting messages, the importance of 'following the thread' and 'focussing in' on the image. Eileen told Jacob of a couple of images she'd received. The first came just before sending out absent healing.

> *I saw three cream cakes and can't understand what they meant, Jacob.*
> What were you thinking about when you saw these cream cakes?
> *Nothing. I had my eyes closed and was about to send out distant healing when I saw them very clearly.*
> How many people were you sending the healing to?
> *I send it to everybody that asks for healing.*
> But which particular people where you focussed upon?
> *Well I usually start with the people who have cancer.*
> How many people are there?
> *Three.*
> Three cream cakes. You see, I know from his mind (the medium) that cream cakes are not an apt symbol in your modern world but in the old days cream would have been a symbol for health. Good milk, good cream, richness, and goodness. So you send three cream cakes out, one for each person. It's a good symbol of giving health and vitality. You see—you've just got to follow the thread.
> *It's not that easy to do.*
> It's very easy; you've just got to think laterally for this deciphering of the messages.

Jacob continued with a personal message for Eileen at the same time using this to re-emphasise his point about lateral thinking. He told her:

> I get a deer for you. You must have confidence because deer are sure of foot. They can bounce around all over the place and not lose their footing. You must be sure of your footing because *you* have good

footing too in healing. Good nose too—intuition. *Think flexibly you see.* You have heard of this **lateral thinking**. You must all develop this lateral thinking for this deciphering of the messages.

Eileen continued and described another image she'd received. She told Jacob:

On another day I was given a dart in my hand; can you interpret that for me, Jacob?
Well you must stay focussed upon your goal and aim straight and true.
Is that regarding mediumship, or something else?
It is to do with life in general, whatever you see as your target, see it true and straight. This is the point though: Do not try to throw too many darts at once. Remember—you were given a **single** dart. You see, even when you get a simple image it is rich in its texture, in its meaning. So the fact that you were given a single dart is of significance. This is important to remember when you get your images; that *if you were given* **one** *dart, there was a reason why you were* **not** *given six.*

Therefore, you must be flexible in your thinking about the images that you receive and see what associations they form for your mind, for they are given with *your* mind, (laughs) in mind. *They are given knowing the associations that you create in your mind.* So you must try to interpret them according to your own interpretation. I can help you in these sessions but you must develop your **own** orientation, **own** interpretation, **own** skill, which you will, as you practise. And as you practise we, in spirit, become more practised in what to give you because we have greater understanding and confidence in how you will read it and interpret it.

Getting the most from your Images

Our daughter, Emma had received an image whilst meditating. She'd got a good understanding of the meaning of this particular image; however, as Jacob pointed out, there was more to her image than she'd realised. Emma told Jacob:

I saw a fence and a horse jumping over it, also the crescent of a moon.

What did you feel about this, Emma?

Well I thought that the fence was an obstacle and the horse was there to help me jump over it. I'm not sure what the moon meant.

Yes you are right, you are right that the fence is an obstacle and you are given a horse to help you jump over it, but there is more to it than this. You like horses, I know, so jumping over the fence is not only *jumping over the fence* but it is a **happy** jumping over the fence.

Yes it was a proper gallop.

So it is *happiness,* and you may take faith, bravery and hope in all this, because you will jump over the obstacles, and you will do so *happily* with a sense of achievement, pride, and happiness. You are given the moon as further confirmation of this. It is a link with the nursery rhyme. There is only one thing missing from it. (Laughs) Yes. The horse jumps over the fence and the cow jumps over the moon. (Laughter) So it is a further indication of happiness, happy things. (Smiles) So you must be *happy* in this.

Note: The significance of this message was understood later when a few weeks before her finals at University, Emma came down with mumps. She was given a two-week extension to hand in her final work but as this took her right up to her final exam she had just two days to revise. It must have felt to Emma, who by now was exhausted, just like she was struggling to complete that final hurdle. Just like Jacob had foretold; with a great sense of achievement, pride, and happiness, she made it, and completed the 'race.'

*   *   *

Eileen asked Jacob about an image she'd received of an actress who in the past had taken part in a well known 'Soap.' The actress is still on the earth plane. The communication below is printed here at Jacob's request.

Eileen told Jacob:

I got a clear image of a well-known actress, Jacob. She no longer takes part in the programme. I thought perhaps she'd passed over but apparently not and

I have no reason to think about her. Why did I get her picture if she's still on the earth plane?

It is possible that you have connected with her while she is still on this plane or you could have connected to someone who is related to her, who wants to demonstrate this connection to you by giving her image to you.

Well I haven't watched the programme for years.

Well then, this is better evidence, is it not. Someone has connected to you and perhaps this person feels some kind of affinity to you; they have happened upon you on their journey and decide to give you an impression. It can happen this way sometimes. There are many travellers moving through your space in the spirit world at any one time. Therefore, they may happen upon you and may convey an impression to you.

There was a pause and Jacob continued:

> We say to you again, my friends, the importance of *feeling* and *emotion* in your connection with us. It is not that you must get all gushy or anything but we connect with you at a feeling level, an emotional, vibrational level. So if you reach out to us in loving feeling compassion then we are assisted greatly in connecting with you.

'Olfaction:' *The sense of smell*

During the same session another member commented:

I regularly get a certain smell and feel it comes from spirit.
What are you connecting with, my friend?
It's a very strong, sweet smell.
Are you aware of any particular person when you receive this smell?
No, but it's the same smell every time.
So you would appear to be connecting with one person, or one group of people perhaps, who convey this energy to you. Have you managed to form any other impressions yet?
Not yet.

Well if you watch and wait you will see, I think. It is rare this gift of 'olfaction,' Carol, so you must develop it, not at the expense of other things, but it is useful that you try to develop it. But you will find that when you grow accustomed to the smells from the spirit world you will also become aware of other impressions, perhaps through sight, hearing or through feeling. In other words, when you connect with the smell, (smiling) the spirit messenger will also convey a message with it. It will come, in a manner perhaps that you will not fully be aware of or understand, but it will develop as you attune to it.

Do I get this because I don't usually have a normal sense of smell?

No, not particularly so. It is something that many people *can* develop, but they do not often develop it, because it is one of the more subtle means of communication and they do not know what to do with it. It is easier of course if you have an association with a particular smell, so if you get that smell you know whom the person is. However, if you get an unfamiliar smell you won't usually understand its meaning so people just say; "Oh I've got an unusual smell," but don't know what to do with it. But as I say, if you attune to that smell, if you focus upon it, eventually you will get some impression of what the person wishes to convey, or who the person might be; so it is an interesting skill to develop.

How children present themselves when they communicate

On another night Jacob was asked:

Is it true that when a child dies it will still grow?

Yes and they have helpers to help them grow. The rate of development may vary. Sometimes it may be speedy and at others it may be slower depending upon the soul and their needs. So you should not necessarily think of a soul being taken back to the spirit world at birth, or even before birth, and then going through that pattern of development as they would on the earth plane. For some it may be very similar, for they may go through the stages of growth and development mirroring, to a point, what they would have experienced on the earth plane. But for others, who are perhaps an evolved advanced soul, the pace of development may be much more accelerated.

What form will they take when they communicate?

They will come to you in a form in which you will recognise them that you may connect with the impression they give in a meaningful way so that you can make sense of it.

How to deal with mischievous spirits

The same person asked:
Jacob, is an aggressive spirit harmful?
You must be careful and exercise discretion in such a case. You will not normally attract spirits who are aggressive, or mischievous if you do not reach out in that way. However, a spirit may sometimes give you a sense of anger because they wish to convey to you that this was a characteristic of their life, or their temperament, or that they were angry about a particular condition or person which they had contact with. If this is the case then they are trying to convey something useful, such as an indication of a relationship perhaps, which they might regret. They may also create an impression of mischief simply to indicate that they were a mischievous soul when on this earth and they were prone to playing practical jokes.

But you will soon recognise whether the spirit concerned is conveying something of this nature, or is a spirit who is truly aggressive and mischievous in a nasty way now. If you should inadvertently contact such a spirit you will very quickly know this.

I have done and wondered what to do.
You must shut down straight away. You must not encourage communication with such souls, for it is unhealthy and unhelpful. If they reform themselves and approach you in a more positive way then you can have communication with them. If you sense anything untoward about them, you should not encourage communication; especially not on your own.

This is a difficult area because we know that all of you do reach out in loving compassion, you reach out with good intent, but you see this is where you must be careful. So we cover **ethics** here again. If you have a row with your beloved spouse, (laughs) for instance, or with your children, with some resulting unpleasantness and you then straight away, without doing anything else, connect with spirit; what do you think will happen?

Like will attract like.

Yes, because although fundamentally you are wishing for the good, the true, the well intentioned, if you have created an emotional bridge, an emotional vibration of a different order *for that instant*, and you then connect at an inappropriate time before you have time to regain your equilibrium, there is a possibility that you may connect with a less savoury character. There is no big danger in this, like I said before, because you will instantly recognise them for what they are and you will pull back; but why bother to go through the trouble? So, following any unpleasantness, you would be better to bring yourself back to inner calm and peace and *only then* reach out to the spirit world.

And you can tell them to go away, can you?

It is best to ignore them. It is like—you bring down a big rod, (smiling) which is a symbol, but then you just ignore them. Do not get into a pattern of saying, "Go away, I don't want to talk to you," because then they may ask, "Why do you not want to talk to me, you are supposed to be a nice person," and if you reply again they get a reaction. They see you are disturbed and if they manage to agitate you they will notice and continue because they enjoy this. So it is simple; just ignore them and go quietly quiet.

*   *   *

The communication below was given to us just as this book was ready for publication. Jacob made a special request for its inclusion, so we have agreed to his request and included it below.

One night, after one member of the group gave details of an image he'd received, Jacob offered him the following advice:

You should approach this image with feeling. You follow me: to **feel** it. This is important; because when we talk about the images that we receive, we will sometimes approach them through our *thinking*; our thought processes, but we may also approach them through our *emotion* of *feeling*. For you, my friend, it is important to develop, the approaching of images, through *feeling*. You have no difficulty in approaching them through *thinking* but you should also try to further develop the *feeling* approach.

Jacob stopped to ask Eileen if this communication could be included in the book; then added for all of us:

When looking at images, you can approach them, either through thinking or feeling, (emotion) and it's important to be open to these different aspects. Many of you may connect in one particular way more easily than the other. Some of you will find it easier to develop the *thinking* side more strongly, while others may it find it easier to *feel*. But it is useful ultimately, to try to *blend the two,* and when you are sufficiently refined, you will find that you are open to **both** ways of approaching the image **simultaneously**. There is a Oneness, in fact, in the way that you *feel* and *think* the image at the same time; *a blending of the two.* This is because you may pick up different things; on the thought wavelength or the feeling wavelength, and by combining the two you will get a fuller and richer picture; a more whole and complete picture.

Chapter 17

Hai & Jonathan

And finally, for the last chapter in part two of this book, we've included two communications from the very early days. The first is from Hai when he took us through 'our paces' for mediumship development. The Phoenix group were still trying out various spirits, who were interested in helping us to develop, to find the one that was the 'best fit' for us. Hai, as usual, opened the session and responded to the various questions put to him. It was time now to move on with the mediumship part of the evening and Eileen asked Hai if there was a spirit available who could assist. Surprisingly, Hai responded by informing us that he would take the session this time.

Following on from Hai another spirit, Jonathan, came through in the customary role of guest speaker; however, after talking for some time about other aspects of mediumship, he indicated that he also would like to give us a couple of exercises to assist in our development.

Hai, on a previous occasion, had decided to change the routine by taking us for a meditation himself, instead of Isleen, and we think that he just likes to 'personally' try things out with us from time to time. However, it is also possible that Hai was simply 'holding the fort' until Jon arrived.

Positive Symbolism
Interpreting Communications

HAI

Hai began:
We shall practise giving messages tonight. We ask you to go deep within yourselves, deep within yourselves, into your quiet. Please

make your minds blank but alert and receptive. But first we want you to simply focus your minds and let all thoughts of your waking day go. As they arise just note them and let them go and practise this please until you achieve a stillness, and when you achieve a quiet stillness just rest in this stillness but be alert to what may come. The purpose of this is that first you must create some space so that what may come, may come from spirit rather than your own mind.

After a few minutes, Hai asked us to come back, but before asking for feedback he commented:

Well now it does not matter what you have received, what you have seen, heard, or smelt. You may have received a message from a loved one, your loved one, or a loved one of someone in this room. You may also have received an inspirational message of peace or an image showing a scene. It does not matter what you've received but please share it with us so that we may all learn. For what is given to one is given to all, that all may learn.

Feedback:

Hai asked for feedback. One member of the group began:

I got a Sycamore tree, which turned to gold.
The sycamore tree is prolific, is it not? The sycamore tree is strong for it has many seedlings. It is not easily eradicated, but grows again through its seedlings and conquers the earth, populates the earth. This is a good image and you may scatter the seeds of your wisdom, your love, in the same way as the sycamore tree scatters its seeds and its seedling grow and become tall strong trees.

Hai continued:
This is true for all of you, my friends, that if you place your kind thought here, your kind look there, your concern here, your thought there, you will find that these will take root in the hearts of others and they will grow into strong trees, for they have been nourished and watered by your hand.

Hai asked Eileen for her feedback. She replied that she'd got nothing. Hai had the following to say about 'nothing'.

> Nothing is a lot. It is rare to have nothing. If you truly have nothing you would be enlightened before long.

Eileen, missing for the moment the point that Hai was making, continued:

> I started to count backwards in the end but you called us back before I could get anything.

Hai replied:
> It's an interesting notion counting backwards.
> Well I was told at a development class that this was a good way to go into meditation.

Hai continued with what he seems to enjoy doing most, which is, helping us to achieve enlightenment.

> This is true because of association of your mind. When you count backwards it's like—*your mind is stepping deeper into the pool*. This is true. But at a deeper level if you meditate upon counting backwards and *what this means*, your mind may be brought to a full stop and maybe it will make a tool for enlightenment. For what is counting backwards? On a superficial level it may mean something, on a deeper level it may mean nothing; therefore, the mind comes to a halt in the struggle, in its attempts to understand it, and when the mind comes to a halt you have enlightenment.

Hai then asked, Jane, another member of the group for feedback. She answered:

> *I got a sailing ship with guns.*
> What do you feel about this image?
> *It was a ship, which might have been preparing for a battle.*
> Do you think the ship was preparing for a battle?

Yes it looked that way, like you see on old films and they show all the guns ready.
Are your guns ready? Who are they aimed at, Jane?
I don't know.
Better you know to outmanoeuvre your foe, to outmanoeuvre your enemy by skill, by using skill of wind and currents. Save your ammunition.

Hai went on to say that he was fascinated with this sailing ship. He asked:

What else did you get with this sailing ship?
The sailors were there standing by the guns.
Did you sense any spirit person connection with this ship?
No, I couldn't see anything else except the sailors.
Therefore, why prepare for battle if there were no other ships?

The message seemed to have meaning in Jane's personal life in that she had been preparing for trouble (battle) unnecessarily.

Hai explained:
Well you should use wind and currents and skirt around and weave around your foe. Elusiveness will make your follower grow tired. Only use head on bombardment when least expected, if you feel battle is necessary.

*   *   *

JON

Jon's communication initially covered a range of topics relating to the development of mediumship. As the discussion tailed off Jon indicated that he would like to give us a couple of exercises, which he referred to as 'experiments.' The Spirit Group have always told us that everything we do is an experiment; some work others don't.

After the first exercise, Jon indicated that the 'experiment' was not their best. Nevertheless, we decided to print the full transcript here because it is interesting and does demonstrate quite well, that although a spirit may give the same image to a number of mediums, the way in which the medium might 'see' the image can vary enormously. However, this does not mean that the *basic* interpretation will necessarily be different.

In the feedback following this exercise you will see that each group member received a different image and Jon uses these images to bring us a message of love and unity. Note how Jon brings out similar aspects from all the images and ties it all together.

Exercise:
Conveying an image

Jon finished his 'talk' and said:

> Let us now try and practise something. I have an image in my mind, which I will try to convey to you in whatever form you may apprehend it, for you may apprehend it in a form which I am not projecting directly, but which you may interpret and pick up in your own way. Therefore, I will project this thought form, this image and we shall see what you receive.
>
> I ask you to blank your minds, to make your minds blank-slates and *receptive*. They need to be blank but receptive. So make your minds *receptive* but put aside any thoughts that you may have and allow the quietness, stillness, and blankness of your mind to take a hold over you for a brief moment. We will then see what image starts to form within your mind.

Jon left us for a few minutes. He then asked that we all give feedback before he told us the image he'd sent.

Feedback

Eileen

> *I received a white wooden watermill.*
> What did you *feel* about this watermill?
> *I'm not sure, but I saw a picture of the countryside with the windmill painted and working with the water.*

Andrew

I saw an old tree and some bamboo furniture.

Duncan

I saw a macaw parrot.

Jon asked:
   And what of this parrot?
   It seemed to have great dexterity i.e. eating whilst holding on.

Kate

I saw a tiger in some undergrowth. It went away and another came. I also saw a crocodile and mallard duck. I felt very calm.

Jane

I was shown either an ice cream cone or a torch of the same shape. Also saw a tree with a holly leaf that was flattened at the base. Then saw a spot light.

Jon then told us:

Well I do not regard this experiment as one of the best; nevertheless, I will tell you what I gave to the medium (Paul.) I gave to this medium a toad. But it is no ordinary toad because it is made of diamonds and beautiful gems gleaming in the light, iridescent in the light. This toad was looking at him with his beady eye, looking at him as your **tiger** looked at you, Kate, and this toad had the appearance of something like the appearance of a tiger. However, I do not want to stretch it too far, for it was all clothed in these gems and gleaming precious metals. I would say the connection is better with the **undergrowth** which many of you spoke of, for the toad is a creature of the undergrowth; a creature that hides between, within, underneath, the trees.

But there was a bigger theme here; for a toad is a detestable creature is it not, to many at least, but we present it here as a creature of beauty. And so we give a paradox here. We give a paradox of this despicable creature presenting itself as a creature of great beauty, of great attractiveness.

Kate commented on the beauty of the macaw. Jon answered:

> Yes just so. There is beauty in this creature but we would say to you, if we stripped this toad of all its precious gems we have uncovered its **true** beauty; you follow me? For the beauty of life is in the eye of the beholder and if we have the eye to behold beauty we will see the beauty in all things, in its wondrous nature. Therefore, you have seen the beauty and magnificence of your macaw, with dexterity of claw, its cleverness of sight, and this is a particular kind of beauty for it's a beauty of its nature is it not. Apart from the beauty of its colours there is a beauty of nature here and we present you with the same image of this toad. There is a beauty of quiet nature here. There is a harmony, a Oneness between these things to an extent, for they partake of nature, a quiet still nature.
>
> The furniture you received, Andrew, **bamboo**, the natural world of the animal kingdom. There is harmony in this. Your **waterwheel**, Eileen, was a waterwheel of the water and truly without water toads could not live and procreate. They connect the earth and the water elements, for it is in the connection of the earth and water elements that life will thrive and persist upon this earth. Without this connection of the water and earth elements there is no life, as we know it. Therefore, you my friends, have focused upon objects of beauty, but the **message** here is that *you should find the beauty within ugliness.*
>
> Like I said before, we do not regard this experiment as one of our most successful, but there is some harmony, purpose of message here.

Mediumship Training

Following on from the above exercise the group had some questions for Jon. Jane began by expressing a concern that she sometimes has difficulty in making her mind go blank. Jon replied:

> Well if you are too busy (in her mind) we will have difficulty in slipping our 'package' in.

What do you do when you train a medium? Do you keep giving them things to find out how they will interpret them?

That is one way, for you all have your own language and interpretation. You will pick up on certain images in certain ways and interpret them accordingly. Therefore, we must be aware of this and work with you through this mechanism, in spite of this, for we cannot assume that you will interpret a tree, a stream, or whatever we give you, in the same way as the next person. We must learn to appreciate how you will interpret these symbols and make sense of them.

I imagine that the medium's guide would eventually be able to do that but what about other spirits who give messages to the medium? Do they do it through the guide or independently?

They may have other helpers around who can assist them in the interpretation. We have our translators, as you have yours. Therefore, we may work with these spirits. They are not alone and isolated you know.

Exercise:
Interpreting Symbols

In the following exercise Jon shows us how to interpret our images by *blending* them to enhance their meaning. Jacob also talks about *blending* images in an earlier chapter.

Jon began:

Let us practise once more but this time you will determine your own image. You will receive your image from someone who may wish to connect with you or from your deeper self.

I would ask you once again to rest your mind; it is better sometimes to think of this analogy of resting your mind, stilling your mind, with this thought of resting it. Do not busy it; let it take a rest (smiling) and while it takes a rest it may be that we, or someone else, may be able to slip the 'package' in of a scene or thought, emotion or smell.

Jon left us again for a few minutes before asking for feedback.

Feedback

Jane

I saw an eagle, and a stone wall with trees on the other side. Stone steps were set in the wall.
What did you make of this Jane?
It was very nice and peaceful.
What connection is the eagle to the stone steps?
Going upwards, in flight.

Jon encouraged Jane to use a blending technique to get the most from her message. He told her:

You must connect the eagle and the steps in a more *blended* way.
Well the steps can take you up but there is a limit. The eagle doesn't have a limit it can sore.
No. It is not about limit.
I can't think of another connection.
Now we must *blend* the eagle and steps. Imagine the characteristics of the eagle, what the eagle may accomplish, but *blend* it with the steps.
Does it mean getting to where you want to get either by flight or other means?
All these things are very true but you have not *blended* the eagle with the steps.
Does it mean that the steps are hard and solid?
No. You are *contrasting* the eagle and steps; you must *blend* the eagle and the steps.
Is it something to do with the steps being firm underneath?
You dwell on the steps and do not *blend* the energies of the eagle and steps.

Jon decided to put Jane out of her misery and told her:

With your own efforts, **stepping one by one** you may **sore high**. This of course *blends* the two energies rather than *contrasting* them.

Andrew

I saw blue sky with clouds. I thought I saw Jesus and was shown a lamb.
You have seen an Enlightened One. One who holds the lamp for others that they may be shown the way. This is what is important in this. Whether it is Jesus or not, is not of any consequence, for you have seen an Enlightened One.

Eileen

I saw the bottom part of something, possibly a cross upside down studded with red rubies.
How do you know if it was a cross if you couldn't see the top?
I just felt it was a cross and when I asked if I could see all of it, I got a tiny pearl which seemed to be set in gold.
Where was this pearl in relation to your cross?
It came straight after.
Was it on its own?
Yes
This is a sword of wisdom with no blade. A sword of wisdom with no blade with which you may make incisive cuts, benevolent cuts, with your pearl of wisdom. There is energy in this sword, this hilt of rubies. There is power in this. The energies are power, love, and wisdom all in one. What a force, what a force to move mountains with.

Jon continued for the rest of the group:

You have such a power with your love my friends, such a power with your love and your wisdom and your hearts; an irresistible power, an irresistible quiet energy, benevolent energy, an energy that can penetrate through to the hearts of others.

Eileen said it was time to finish and Jon responded by giving us his blessing.

*   *   *

All ends are new beginnings; therefore, we will bless you with your newly found sword of loving energy. We would knight you one by one with the blessing of this sword. Arise my sires and ladies. Our love goes out to you.

Part 3

Meditation & Its Value

Chapter 18

Development through Meditation

Both Hai and Isleen have told us that guided meditations are a useful tool, both as an aid for the development of mediumship, and for our spiritual unfoldment. One night a member of our Home Circle asked Isleen if she would take us through a meditation. She willingly obliged and so our regular meditation evenings were born.

Following the meditation, Isleen will always ask for feedback and will help us to interpret the images we receive. She often gives us explanations about what she wanted to achieve with a particular meditation and is always happy to answer any questions we have. No two meditations have ever been the same.

Below Isleen explains how a guided meditation can facilitate contact with the spirit world. The explanation she gives here is for a particular meditation. However, the general theme would apply equally to the meditations that come later in this section.

Isleen told us:

We work you all hard because we assume you wish it, because you wish to develop and progress. We use the pool in the first instance to transport you to this beautiful landscape because it is a process, by which you may enter your imaginations. By entering our imaginations we may enter more and more deeply, just as I suggested when you looked into the pool. The landscape took form slowly, gradually, but evermore vividly and so we give ourselves to the sight, we give ourselves to the landscape, to our imagination, and we enter deeply into this new world.

As we enter deeply into this new world we provide ourselves with the opportunity of gaining access to a world beyond our imagination, to attune and to become at one with the world of spirit and a different reality. So our imaginations and the spiritual are closely intertwined, and we may use our imaginations as a vehicle for making contact with the spiritual, and things and beings of the spiritual.

*   *   *

One night Hai was asked:

Do you scan us before each meditation to find out what our needs are?
We know where your inclinations lay on the night. Sometimes this is because you indicate and portray what you wish within your own words and we can read between the lines to assess your inclination. Other times we have already identified a need from a previous occasion, and therefore, we think this may be of some usefulness to you.
I suppose you know better than us what we need.
No we do not impose; we read the signs and we try to match with your expectations, your wishes, and your needs.
Is it important to meditate?
Meditation is a big help towards mediumship, for it puts your mind in a mindset that greatly facilitates and aids mediumship and the connection with us for communication. Therefore, it is a great aid, a great facilitator.
Is it a good idea to meditate outside sometimes with your eyes open?
It is useful sometimes to meditate outside but perhaps you achieve different results from this form of meditation. It is also helpful to meditate open eyed on nature, over a lake or wide river for example. This is different to meditating with closed eyes but it has its own special value. It helps you to be At One with the natural world, to realise your inherent Oneness with it, the Oneness of all life.

Rules of Meditation

One night Hai was asked a question about the rules of meditation.

Some leaders of meditation groups advise that we should have only minimal or no food before meditating. Is this necessary?

No, it is simply a matter of not having a full stomach. A full stomach will make your mind 'go to your stomach' but otherwise there is no point in starving yourself. So it is what you are comfortable with, what you know from your own experience. This is more important than your rules that you speak of. (Smiles) There should be a happy medium, as in all things.

*   *   *

Auras

On another night Isleen attempted to clarify some misunderstanding about the colours of auras. She began the session by telling us that we were all looking radiant. Isleen was asked how she knew that. She replied:

I viewed with my eyes to see your inner being, your souls.
Aren't we all beings of light anyway?
Yes this is true, John.
Do we radiate different colours?

Isleen laughed and replied:

*It depends upon the lens of your microscope. You must forgive me; I tease you. Yes, we do, to an extent, have different colours, but there are those who dwell upon this too much, for the colours can shift and take different shape and form. What is important though, is that we are **all** golden light in our **essence**. Some would try to disrupt the spirit land by the use of these colours for they would attempt to make a distinction between different people based upon this. This is wrong of course. And if they do this they will not be around that region for long, for they will bring disharmony because they split and distinguish where there should be no distinction. So it is as you said before my friend, that it is simply a matter of being true to our inner selves, of expressing ourselves, the warmth and love and compassion of ourselves, to all around us.*

One member of the group was intrigued by the idea of people in the spirit world arguing about something of this nature. She commented:

It seems strange to think of people in the spirit world arguing about the different aura colours.
They do not argue in the enlightened regions, but on the periphery, in those regions that are neither of the light nor of the grey darkness, then sometimes this can happen.
Are there conflicts in those regions?
Yes there are conflicts and to a point you would ask; (laughs) is this heaven, is this truly the spirit land? But yet there are many variations in the depth of people's love and understanding and this is as it should be, this is as it is because everyone is on a path to enlightenment. Everyone is on a path to their maker, if you wish, and we are bound to be on different points on that journey. Therefore, it is to be expected that people will have different insights, different perceptions from where they are. Therefore, we must have a tolerance and patience for we too have been on the point of path where they are now.
Can drinking water help us to develop spiritually?
Water sustains the physical body, but you may **meditate** upon water to advantage.

*   *   *

It was time to finish and Isleen gave us her blessing before she left.

And so it falls to me to finish. I wish you peace and contentment, peace of mind and joy of heart. These things I wish for you and I leave you now but I hope that we may speak again soon. Please go with our love and care and concern for you. Goodbye.

Chapter 19

Isleen

How to Understand and Use Images in Meditation

The Lotus Flower

During one meditation we were given a lotus flower. Isleen explained later how, when meditating alone, we could use the lotus flower to aid our progress. She told us:

You may use the lotus flower in various ways. You may use it in a simple meditation, a meditation to help you calm and still your mind during the turmoil of your working days. If you can spare a few moments to imagine the petals of the lotus flower opening and follow it as the petals open one by one; stilling your mind, allowing your mind to enter a deeper calm, you may find it of some benefit. For while you focus upon the petals of the lotus flower and follow it methodically you cannot focus upon other things, which trouble you.

You should know also that as the petals open they open to the golden centre, the golden centre of stillness, of vitality of life, of wisdom. This symbolises your own centre and you should take refuge and strength in your centre, your own essence, and your own heart, which is divinely connected with the Great Heart of all.

You should think of a divine light and golden love emanating from within your own hearts and emanating outwards to embrace all, to embrace each other and all things in creation. Remember that you are connected with the Great Heart of all, the Great Heart of the One Mind, which embraces all in its love, in its acceptance, in its support, in its sustenance.

The golden light of the landscape, which you walked through in this meditation, was the golden Mind of love that embraces all, which interpenetrates all, permeates all, and caresses all.

Water

Someone commented that water featured a lot in our meditations and asked whether it was symbolic of anything. Isleen replied:

> Water is symbolic of life, is it not? It is mysterious for it is hard to grasp. You try to grasp it in your hand and it disappears from your grasp. You cannot hold it yet it is fundamental to life. Without it there is no life. It is intangible, yet it is strong, for it will wear down mountains to plains in the course of time. In its apparent softness it has a mighty strength. It is patient, it is enduring, and it finds ways where others cannot follow, where others cannot tread, for it is wise. It finds the crevices of the earth and uses them to its own advantage.
>
> Water has many meanings on different levels, my friend, for we may look at it in different ways. Hai has often told you of the mighty ocean of the One Mind. This ocean contains all, embraces all and it is as if we are little wavelets upon its surface. Insolubly we are part of this mighty ocean, yet we seem to take and manifest our own identity in the form of these little wavelets upon its surface. But these little wavelets never separate from their foundation, their direct entity, their heart, their essence and so it is with us my friend. We are never apart and nor can we make ourselves apart from the One Mind, the One Heart; nor can we separate ourselves from Its love for we are embraced in Its love and caress, for all time.

*   *   *

We've found that, often, the most difficult thing in our meditations is not the 'seeing' of images but working out what those images mean. In this section we've included a small sample of explanations offered to us following one of our many meditation sessions.

The Spirit Group never miss an opportunity to refer to the One Mind and to emphasise their love for humanity. They also use their communications, whenever possible, to teach patience and tolerance to others. You will notice that Isleen has continued with this theme in the transcript below.

The Daisy

One person asked about the significance of a daisy she'd chosen in her meditation. Isleen replied:

> The daisy you chose is of interest for it combines the two qualities of great strength, great radiant power, symbolised by the centre of the daisy. There is a purity of its leaves and petals and there is vast power in its heart and centre. There is great purity of expression symbolised by its petals and this reflects the manifestation of the One Mind. We should all think on this, for we can tap into the great radiant power within the centre of the universe, the essence of all, the One Mind. However, we must be sure to use this power for good, and our motives must be pure in order to achieve this and to benefit mankind and the world in which you live.

The Red Flower

One healer in the group asked about a red flower he'd received. Isleen responded by asking:

> Does your red flower have a golden centre to it?
>
> *Yes I think it has a yellow centre.*
>
> So we have power once more, a reservoir of power, a reservoir of gold and beautiful power that may reach out to the four corners of the universe with its healing energies. The red of the petals of this flower are a gentle red, a gentle energy, which is strong and powerful. And so you may reflect your role as a channel of this strong gentle radiating energy that is given by the One Mind, the Essence of All, which we are inextricably linked to and is our heart; we may radiate its energies to the benefit of our brothers and sisters.
>
> *I wanted to choose another paler coloured one at first. Is there a reason for this?*
>
> You wished a more delicate coloured one? You wish perhaps to transmute your energy into a softer expression sometimes, but you

have an energy, a drive, a power that is valuable. If you wish to transmute it to a more gentle form you must do precisely that; transmute it, but without losing it. You follow me?

I follow you but I don't know how easy that would be for me.

None of our tasks are easy for us; none of our tasks are easy, but there is much to be gained by following the path, by stepping one step in front of the other no matter how hard our goal may seem. We are all plagued by habit, we are all plagued by what we have inherited in our bodies, but we can change our habits, we may unlearn our habits and transmute them. This is not easy but we are to be even more commended when we do.

We are all of us in need of transmuting some parts of ourselves so we would do well to focus upon what change we would like to achieve. However, we do need to be patient with ourselves for if we do not love ourselves we cannot love others. If we cannot be patient with ourselves how can we be patient with others?

Turquoise Blue Flower

Another member asked about a blue flower she'd received in her meditation. Isleen advised her on how she could pass on healing to others:

Your turquoise blue flower perhaps would symbolise the ability of practical wisdom to heal in its own way. By offering those around us practical wisdom we can heal them, we can heal their plight. And by bringing wisdom of the right kind, a healing wisdom, we can heal their relationships with others. You may heal with your spirit energies, with your hands, if you wish, but there are many forms of healing which we may offer our friends, our brothers and sisters.

One form is to offer wisdom, practical wisdom to ease their mind, to ease their plight and troubles and to offer them a skilful way through life's turbulent waters. So your words of wisdom may offer healing to others.

Foxgloves and the Human Soul

Isleen had the following to say when someone in the group received a foxglove in her meditation.

The Foxgloves are strong yet appear fragile, gentle, and vulnerable almost, and yet they stand so erect with their heads held high reaching to the sun. There is a beauty and nobility about them and so there is a nobility and beauty about the human soul, which also in its earthly form is so vulnerable, so fragile. Yet in spite of this we may all hold our heads high, we may all reach to the sun. And in spite of our fragility there is an inner strength in us, an inner ability, a beauty, and we may reach high in our efforts, we may reach high as the foxgloves reach if we have confidence in ourselves, hope in the future and trust in life. If we have or if we cultivate these qualities, we may reach to great heights.

The flowers of the Foxglove are many and flower in turn up the spiral of its stem and as one flower gives way and withers the next blooms. It is like an athlete passing on a batten in a human race; we need the person before us to have done their bit, to have fulfilled their mission and pass on the batten to us for us to carry for a little time. So we do our bit and pass it on again, but we are all dependent on one another. We stand on the shoulders of others and others in turn stand on our shoulders and so we are interwoven in this way, dependent upon each other. And this dependence is a beautiful thing, it is our communion, our brotherhood between us.

*   *   *

It was time to finish and Isleen gave us her blessing.

I would give you our blessing and I would hope you would give us yours, for we are all partners in this. We may be a little further up the mountainside sometimes, amidst the dancing trees, but the path is the path that we must all walk, and we are partners in this. So, I will say goodbye, and I would wish you, particularly, joy of life, joy of heart. Goodbye my friends until we can speak again.

Chapter 20

A Selection of Meditations

In this chapter we've selected two of Isleen's Meditations. They were recorded 'live' on mini disc and then transferred onto a CD or typed up. If you like them you could record one onto a tape and play it back when you want to meditate. We've found that the music, 'Fairy Rings,' by Mike Roland, is an excellent piece of music to play in the background because of its nice calm even tone. Some of Isleen's meditations are available on our website.

Meditation

The Waterfall and the Cave

Isleen began:

I would ask you my friends to breathe slowly in and slowly out; to feel the fresh air filling your lungs and then to let it go quietly and peacefully. Keep doing this and feel a growing peace with all the cares of our world drifting away from you.

I would like you to imagine yourself sitting on the banks of a beautiful lake, a beautiful lake with still waters. The sun is shining on the waters and you can see the reflection of its rays rippling on this beautiful lake. As you cast your eyes around the lake you can see magnificent trees clothing its banks. All around are beautiful, beautiful trees. And as you look down you can see the green grass upon which you sit. It feels so luxuriant, so alive, and vibrant with colour. In the distance you can see swans gliding effortlessly on the waters of the lake. They seem to be coming in your direction, peacefully, so effortlessly. You become aware of a figure approaching you along the bank of the lake.

The person seems to be a 'being of light' for light emits from them. The light shimmers from the glow; it's so beautiful. You think of this 'being' as a beautiful woman and as she approaches, you notice her lovely embracing smile and can feel the healing in her face as she bathes you with her smile. She indicates that you take her by the hand and you know she wishes you to go on a little journey with her.

So you set off along the lakeside, she guides you along the path and you walk slowly along taking in the beauty of the scene as you go. You look about you and see the beautiful shrubs and flowers, which clothe the banks of this lake. In a while the path enters the trees that surround this lake and you continue along the path.

As you enter into the wood you can see the rays of sun coming through the well-spaced trees, which allow the beautiful golden rays to shine through. You carry on and as you look through the trees you see deer raising their heads from grazing, looking at you curiously. The path starts to climb gently and you begin to go up a hillside. You hear a babbling brook and your friends suggests that you stop to listen for a while because you may hear a message and some words of wisdom in it. (Couple of minutes pause)

In a short while you move on to go further along the path and continue climbing slowly. The babbling brook sounds louder and you can hear its waters more clearly. The path starts to level out and there through the trees, you see a silvery pond, a beautiful pond of crystal clear water. As you draw nearer you also see the stream that gushes from it which overflows and makes its way down to the lake. At the far side you become aware of a louder rush of water and you see a beautiful waterfall, which feeds this pool. Your friend points towards this waterfall and you know she wishes you to go over towards it to have a closer look.

You both walk along the side of this beautiful silvery pool, over towards the direction of the waterfall, and you notice that there are some stepping-stones, which can take you through the waterfall beyond and into a cave behind the falls. Your friend goes ahead of you, and carefully, one by one, you step on each stone. You go nearer and nearer to the waterfall and soon you enter the waters. The water feels soft and gentle and is so embracing you can hardly feel it at all. All you can feel is a beautiful energy that seems to radiate through you. So your friend asks you to stop, to wait in the middle of these falls to experience this beautiful energy, for this is healing energy, which will help you. After a short pause, you continue on your way. Eventually you come through the waterfall and find yourself in a silvery cave.

The walls of this cave glisten with silver. They seem alive with the silver light and you are amazed at the beauty. However, your friend does not wish you to pause and draws you further on into the cave, which opens out like a beautiful cathedral. As you walk into its central chamber it truly is like the central nave of a cathedral. A golden light comes down from its roof and radiates in a beautiful golden ray upon the centre of the floor. All around the walls of this 'cathedral' in the cave, you can see interesting sculptures in the wall. You are amazed at the number you can see for the whole of this place is carved with different pictures and scenes and you marvel at the variety of them. You feel drawn to go over and look at one in particular, so you make your way over and cast your eyes over it. You take in all the detail and the *message* it has for you. (Pause)

In a short while your friend beckons you to come over to the centre of this mighty 'cathedral' towards where the golden light shines down upon its floor. She bids you to sit down in the centre of this light and tells you that this centre of golden light is the means of communicating with your own inner being and with the very Essence of Life. So you sit in the golden light. You feel bathed by its love and compassion and wait for communication. (Few minutes pause)

You become aware of your friend once more and you walk over to her feeling refreshed and at ease. She takes you by the hand and together you walk back from where you came. You walk back along the passageway and in a short while you find yourself by the waterfall. You can see the stone steps once more going through the pool and as you pass through it you feel once more its comforting waters and vibration. You reach the path once more and you make your way back along the pool, all the time looking at the beauty of its vegetation. You take the downward path towards the lake once more walking through the trees taking in the scene as you go. You can hear the babbling brook as it so merrily makes its way down to the lake and before long you find yourself back beside the lake.

You follow the path out between the trees, out to the open countryside beyond and onto the grass where you first sat. Your friend smiles at you once more, and, from behind, pulls out a flower for you to take as a gift. You look at the flower and thank her for the gift. You turn, say goodbye, and see her turn back along the path, back towards the forest. You sit down beside the lake once more, the flower in your hand, looking across the waters of the lake. The sun is lower in the sky and the waters are beautiful and golden. There is such a feeling of peace and tranquillity.

Slowly the scene recedes from your sight and you start to become more aware of the room in which you sit. You become more aware of yourself and your feet upon the floor, of your hands and your body, and slowly, slowly, when you are ready, open your eyes.

Meditation

The Native American Village

I would ask you to breath in slowly and deeply, filling your lungs with air and as you fill your lungs with air, slowly and gently, you feel refreshed and invigorated. And as you expel the air from your lungs you feel all the cares and troubles of your earthly life depart from you. Feel them melting away as if they are snow in a brilliant bright sun. As you breathe in the fresh invigorating air again you feel so well, so recharged, and as you breath out you feel a deeper and deeper peace and calm entering your mind.

I would ask you now to imagine yourself beside a magnificent lake of clear water. Its waters reflect the sun in the sky, which is radiating a gentle light over the waters of the lake. And as you look around you, you see magnificent forests all clothing the edges of this beautiful majestic lake, and in the distance you see mighty mountain peaks rising up through the forest. The peaks are clothed in brilliant white snow, and as you look on the scene you marvel at the beauty of the country and at the majesty of the scene before your eyes.

You decide to take a closer look at this lake so you head towards the shore, but as you walk along you become aware of another person ahead, sitting quietly by the lakeside. You continue along the shore and as you approach, it is as if the person knows that you are there for he turns to look in your direction. You recognize an Indian soul, a Native American Indian man who looks towards you with such knowing eyes of love and compassion that you feel perfectly safe and comfortable with him. You move closer and he holds out his hand in welcome. He tells you he is glad that you have visited his homeland and says that he would like to take you to his village, which is a short distance away. You agree to his kindness and follow him to his home.

Off you go together, away from the lake, into the forests and you follow a small path that takes you through the mighty pines and fir trees. As you continue you become aware of all the animals that live in this mighty forest. You see squirrels jumping through the trees and deer skipping along. You see bears in the distance but they are no trouble to you for they are going about their lives seeking food. You feel so well, so at ease, you feel a deep sense of belonging with this forest, a deep sense of comfort from its trees, and so you follow your friend further on down the trail.

In a short time you see the trail opening out into a large clearing and all around this clearing you see Indian tepees, the village home of your friend. Your friend tells you that he will take you to meet some of the important people in his village. He would like you to meet them because they may provide you with some assistance. And so he points over to a large tepee which is clothed in hides and has all kinds of interesting images drawn upon the outside of the tepee. You make particular note of an image that attracts your attention and you go on with your friend and approach the entrance to this tepee.

Your friend calls inside and out of the tepee comes a great chief clothed in a magnificent headdress. His eyes seem to dance when they reach yours and there is an instant welcoming smile for you. Your friend explains that you have come for a visit. The chief bids you sit down opposite him and asks if you have any question that concern you, which he might advise you on. For he says,
"I am old and wise and have lived in these forests for many years. I am connected with spirit so I may be able to advise you on your concern."
And so you think about this for a minute and you decide on a question that you will pose to this mighty chief. You then silently listen to what the chief will say in response. (Few minutes pause)

You receive the chief's words, thank him for his kindness, and bid each other farewell. Your friend now indicates that he has another friend who could be of service to you and he points across to another tepee at the far side of the village. This time you see a magnificent buffalo head on a pole outside this tepee. Your friend once again calls inside and an Indian man comes out with another impressive buffalo head on his head and again his eyes radiate compassion and understanding.

Once more you are bid to sit down outside the tepee and he tells you.
"I am the medicine man of this village and I am skilled in the ways of healing. I am skilled in the ways of using the energies of the earth to bring about good and beneficial means."
He asks you if there is any healing you require, either for yourself or someone else. He tells you that healing is his area of skill and explains that he may heal in different ways. He says, 'I may heal the soul, I may heal the spirit, I may heal the emotions. Convey to me what concern you have for yourself or another and I will do what I can to advise you to bring about healing.' So once more you pose your question and then you listen to what the medicine man has to say. (Few minutes pause)

In a little while, when you have heard what the medicine man has to say, you look into his kind eyes and thank him for his words and thoughts. Once more you bid farewell to your new friend and you turn to your guide. Together you get up and walk back across the village. Your friend tells you he will now guide you back to the lakeshore; so, off you go along the path towards the lake. You walk again through the mighty trees of the forest and you see the animals going about their lives quietly. Once more you feel a sense of belonging, a oneness with this place. In a little while you see water again through the trees, and eventually you find yourself beside the majestic, beautiful lake.

Your friend tells you he is most pleased you were able to visit his village today and says he will give you a gift to remember him by; you open out your hand and he places his gift in it. You look at it and offer your thanks. He then says it is time to return to your home but adds also that you may return to him at any time you wish. You have only to think of the forest and the lakeside and he will be there to guide you. So you thank your friend and turn back along the direction from where you first came, looking back once more to give him a final wave of farewell.

You make your way along the lakeside back to the spot from which you started. You sit down for a minute or two on a small boulder and reflect upon your experiences this day. Slowly, slowly you become more aware of your room, more aware of the seat in which you are sitting, and when you are ready still feeling totally relaxed, at ease and calm, slowly open your eyes.

*   *   *

Isleen later told us that she'd chosen the meditation above because of a particular circle member's interest and concern for the earth. She continued:

The meditation conveyed a deep harmony between those who live on the earth and the nature of the earth; a deep harmony of life between the natural world, the human beings, and the animals who live within the world. So we would hope that you will take this vision of deep harmony and peace and oneness, away with you, and it will provide you with strength in your endeavours.

*   *   *

Someone commented that she had felt very calm during the meditation and Isleen went on to say:

This is good; for this is one of the main purposes of the meditation; to bring about calm and relaxation, a calm state of mind. For if you can achieve a calm, serene state of mind, you open yourself to the possibility of communication from other worlds, from spirit.

Part 4

A selection of Spirit Guest Speakers

Chapter 21

James

James' Message:
There is no need to feel 'honoured' by your Guide's presence

James visited us following one of our meditation sessions, which we'd put on especially for a particular group of people. Isleen, when taking us through our meditations, is particularly softly spoken, and two people in the group, who had a slight hearing difficulty, commented that they couldn't always hear her.

James' voice, on the other hand, was loud, clear, and precise. He made a joke about being pushed to the front of the crowd (spirit crowd) by Davia, our spirit gatekeeper, because his voice would be of particular use to us that night.

James presents with a humorous forthright personality. He talks about communication with the spirit world and offers his opinion on the relationship between our guides and us. James' humour is particularly in evidence when he offers a humorous view of Davia's 'stage management' skills.

Why Guides Communicate

One member of the group, Peter, asked:

Why do we on the earth plane, have so much contact with spirit guides?

James laughed and replied:
 Well, Peter, would you rather we did not bother you? You must understand my dear friend; we are all of one Community. Your friend asked Hai, a short while ago, about God, the Essence. Well, we are all

of the Essence. We are all of the same Divine Community, we are all of the Brotherhood, the Sisterhood; whatever you wish to call it. We are all of one, Oneness, One Suchness with each other. We are all joined together. Therefore, does it not seem reasonable to you, Peter, that we would wish to stay in contact with you all while you are on your earthly sojourn. We care and are concerned about you.

You picked up in your meditation, feelings of love, of comfort and warmth, and we try to convey these feelings to you when you enter a meditative state. And the deeper you enter such a meditative state the deeper is the opportunity to connect with you and to relay these feelings of love and oneness with you, because it is a shared experience. It is not only that we wish to reach out to you but also we know that you wish to reach out to us, for you sense the Oneness, you sense the Togetherness and you sense the Divine Brotherhood that exists between us all.

And so it is only natural, if you have made a close friend and you do not see this friend for some time, you may well feel; "Oh I would like to see so and so again," and you would be prepared to make the effort to see your friend again. So my dear friends we must all make the effort to connect with each other, and if we wish this to happen we all have work to do. Some feel it is not worth the effort but there are many like yourselves who feel it *is* worth the effort and it is effort on *your* side my friends as well as effort on *our* side. It truly is a reaching out and a bridging of the imaginary divide which divides us, that we may connect with each other, that we may share moments together, that we may share love together.

You know, there are thousands of spirits gathered around where communication takes place. It is as if a mighty beacon has been put up for all to see, and all gather around out of interest to see what might take place. And therefore, my friend with the paddle (reference to 'gatekeeper', Davia) tends to pick out those from the crowd whom he feels may serve some particular purpose on that particular occasion.

You see that I have been gifted by this booming voice. I have floated to the surface of this mighty crowd because of my booming voice, which my friend with the paddle has noticed, and thought; "Ah you shall do for tonight my friend; you are ideal for my purpose." (Laughing) You see how he abuses us my friends. On another occasion he would cast us onto the drift of the waves if we do not suit his purpose, but on the present occasion he has found that I, humble James, suit his purpose and he has dragged me in. (This brought about more laughter) So on this occasion I am useful but on another occasion he will fling me to the back of the queue.

I wondered whether in communicating with spirit we harm your progress?

No you will not harm our progress, Peter. You must have no cause for concern on that account. I would say to you however, that the most important thing in this, as in other things, is what Hai was saying to you earlier on. What is important in this is good intent. If your intent is of a good nature; if you are of benevolent disposition; if you seek communication for good ends, ends which could be of benefit to all concerned, then you need have no fear on any account that it will trouble or inconvenience us in any way whatsoever. And indeed the very fact that you give us opportunities to speak means that you may *aid* our progress rather than hindering it, because by enabling us to communicate with you, you enable us to be of service to you in our own humble way. Therefore, in doing this you are enabling us to act out our karma, you are enabling us to promote our own progression, and indeed, at the same time, hopefully aiding your progression. So all our purposes are served, we would hope, in great measure and you must have no concern on this account.

The other thing to note in this, and it is a point for all of you; is that when you are thinking of loved ones you should, where possible, think of them with warmth, with love, and with compassion. It also helps to think of them with gentleness, with an untroubled mind and heart and with memories of gladness and of happiness. Can you understand the reason for this? Because if you were to constantly reach out to your loved ones or those you've been acquainted with, with feelings of remorse, feelings of sadness, of regret, then you send up those emotions to them and this may cause them some discomfort and concern. You see, they are open to your feelings because when we are in spirit we are indeed more receptive to feelings than when we are in the earthly frame, and therefore, any feelings which you reach out with, we feel more intensely than you do on the earth.

Therefore, feelings from you, of remorse, regret, and discomfort, we can feel in great measure and does not serve any useful purpose. It would instead serve the purpose of agitation. So I would encourage you, although it is natural that you will sometimes feel sadness, but overall I would encourage you to feel warmth, to feel happiness and rejoice in the memories of your dear ones who have passed over to our side. And in reaching out in this vein you will attract them to you and you may join for a moment in harmony and happiness.

Form in the spirit world
Communication with each other and guides

What form do you take on the spirit side, James?

The form I take is of an energy form, which *we* see as a bodily form as assuredly as I see your bodily form. Therefore, we are of energy primarily but we may take a form of energy, we may express our energy in a form of a bodily image. So I say to you once more, that although there are differences in the spirit plane there are many similarities, and indeed in expressing ourselves here there is much similarity to our earthly manifestation.

We do not though, have the limitations that you have in your earthly form. We may communicate by means of thought and by means of feeling, and this assuredly is as clear, as valid and as deep a means of communication as any communication that you convey through your words of your mouth. Our thoughts are quicker; feelings also are as lightening and in being able to convey feelings we are able to convey much more than mere thoughts.

The thoughts and feelings of course may merge and blend with each other as we convey something. But you understand the distinction I make here; because you on your earth could convey thought but the thought would be in the form of an idea, a concept, or something of this nature, but if you could also convey feeling, emotion with that thought, theory, concept or idea then obviously your communication would be ten times stronger. And this is what we are capable of in the spirit world.

While still on this plane (earth) you may become capable of this in some measure. Indeed Paul (the medium) has some experience of communicating with Isleen and Hai through emotion and feeling, through connecting with each other for a brief moment in time, and it was of such intensity that it has stayed with him to a great degree even to this day. It is a very real experience, a very strong experience. So you on the earth plane, may also develop this skill, to an extent, but I fear not to the extent to which you will practice it when you are in the spirit body.

One member of the group said she was very honoured that her guide used her for automatic writing. James' reply was interesting.

> You do him honour also—and I would like to make this point to you once again because it touches and reconnects once more with what I said before. I was asked whether you interfere in any way by seeking our company and I answered in the negative. I will say this again to you. Your guide is most gratified that you have provided him with the opportunity to be of inspirational benefit to you, to inspire your writing, and therefore, you should not speak in terms of honour which he does you, for you do him honour likewise by your association; by providing him with the opportunity to be of service to you. It is most important that you know that it is a partnership between us all. I hear so many times of people who speak of being 'honoured;' this is balderdash. So you must be clear on this; that it is a partnership between us, a happy partnership, a partnership which we both delight in, and therefore, this is the way to view it.

Chapter 22

The 'Orchestrator,' WB

We've already printed some of WB's communication in earlier sections of this book. In the early days we were aware that WB was a scientist when last on the earth plane and continues his interest now in the spirit world. We also realised that he took part in the developments when we sit for physical phenomena but didn't know the detail of his role in this. One night Hai was asked:

What does WB do?
WB acts as a monitor, as a controller and an overseer of events. He facilitates these events in the background. He checks on the condition of the medium and he checks on the conditions around you all within the room. He checks the links between the two worlds, so he orchestrates, if you like, in the background. There are many roles in our group and each person contributes in their own way. The roles of some of the others will become clearer in the course of time.

There was a pause, then WB then came through in person and said:

I don't usually get involved in this way but as you have all expressed an interest in seeing me; not that you can see me as such, but you have expressed an interest, so Hai has suggested that I put in a brief appearance. I usually prefer though to stay in the background and do my bit.
It must be a very important bit?
I would not say so but you may say so.
Is the term 'gatekeeper,' connected with the work you do?

I would not call myself a gatekeeper. It is more as Hai said, 'orchestrator'—someone who orchestrates. Yes I like that word; orchestrates. Gatekeeper sounds boring. Gatekeeper sounds like someone who lifts the latch and opens the gate and shuts it again, boring.

Why do you like to be called WB?

It is the way I am accustomed to be called.

Were you an orchestrator of some kind while on the earth plane?

No, the orchestrator is merely symbolic of what I do.

How long ago were you on the earth plane?

Not that long ago really. Not as long ago as the old man, Hai, has been on this side. He's been here much longer than I have, longer than all of us have.

Are all the people in the Phoenix group, of like-mind? Is that why you have come together?

Yes, it is important this, important that we are of like-mind, wishing to share together in the same venture. It is also important for you to be of like-mind on your side of the venture, from the earth plane. If our two 'intents' are in harmony, as they are, then we can link together, we can link together in communion, and the venture is sure of success because there is a loving harmony between us.

Chapter 23

Ada
A light interlude

The following is an example of how someone in spirit, who was known to a person many years ago, may come along simply to say hello. Ada had known Eileen when she was a very young child but, as so often happens, they had lost touch when Eileen had moved away. We decided to print an extract of Ada's visit in this section because she offers some useful information about contact with our loved ones in the spirit world.

Her communication was light hearted and pitted with jokes throughout. She told us that she was no longer with, Jack, her husband, though they kept in touch. Ada said that her main area of work now was with children and she enjoyed this work very much. This did not surprise Eileen at all because her early memories of her were of someone who had a great deal of patience and who loved to interact with children.

Ada talked about how spirit picks up our vibrations when we sit as a group for contact with them. She also gave us other useful information to help with our contact with spirit. As she came through, one member of the group received a clairvoyant image of her and commented:

I got an image of you in the kitchen. Did you like your kitchen when on the earth plane?

Yes I enjoyed doing things in the kitchen. You don't have tables in the kitchen so much these days.

Well not many of the traditional ones, like you would have had.

Don't know how you manage.
We have what we call, work tops.
Yes, we looked at them, not very practical.
Do you have a house of your own in the spirit world?
Oh yes, we all have our little houses.
Does it resemble where you used to live?
Not a lot, no. It's more to our own choosing. Can't always choose, can you, when on the earth plane. Got to put up with things a bit. We've been able to choose a bit more, which is nice. Yes, got to behave ourselves though, so we can choose.
Is it possible to choose your neighbours?
You would not build your house where you would not wish to be. We all get on generally very well anyway. It's not a big problem.
Is that because of the harmony in the spirit world?
Yes, and there are not the pressures here you see. There is much more harmony and give and take.
Do you have lots of flowers in the garden?
Yes there are plenty of flowers, all kinds of flowers, lots of roses and carnations, yes, and other flowers. So many varieties of flowers here, some you know, and some you don't know.

Ada then turned to one of the group and asked:

Do you like flowers my dear?
Oh yes, I love flowers.
What's your favourite flower?
I don't know. I like them all so much. I like lilies very much.
Oh yes, they're lovely aren't they, beautiful, lilies.
Sometimes I buy them for the spirit people.
Yes and they are grateful for that you know; nothing goes unnoticed. Even when you chatter away to them and you think you must be mad, but nothing goes unnoticed. We are grateful for the link.
Can spirit sense the perfume in flowers?
We can sense the perfume. We can sense the colour. We can sense the flower itself. Yes, we can see fine you know.
When you visit relatives on earth, can you see their homes and can you see them as well as when you were on the earth?
Yes, we can, yes.

Is this the first time you've communicated in this way?

Oh yes, it's hard, very hard. I knew I was coming for the 'show.' (Our sitting) I was not sure about this. Even when I was trying to come through I wasn't sure about it.

Were you not sure whether you wanted to do it?

It was about whether I *could* do it.

Does someone on your side help you to come through?

Yes, your spirit friends and guides help. We wouldn't be able to do it without their help.

How did you know about these meetings here?

(Laughing) Oh well, if you will go lighting 'bonfires' you'll attract people and because there is the link between Eileen and me it means that I know when there is a significant bonfire. (The use of the word bonfire was Ada's way of describing the 'light' we send out when we sit)

What is it that creates the light?

You create your energy between you. This acts as a beacon or magnet, call it what you will (smiling) but we know there are 'goings on.'

Eileen Asked:

If just Paul and I sit together, does it have the same affect?

It still acts as a beacon. But the more who gather in harmony the more power there is reaching out.

How many other beacons are there on a Friday night?

Friday night is a rather popular night for these events, but there are other beacons during the week.

Do you attend those as well?

No. I might sometimes have a look, but they are not as significant for me.

One spirit who came through suggested that he was 'doing the rounds.'

(Laughs) Yes, seeing who had the best jokes.

How many beacons are there in the North West?

Ada laughed and asked:
The northwest of what?
Manchester.

There are quite a few. The funny thing is that we know where they all are and you don't. I sometimes bring some of the children with me. They have the spirit of a child, young in spirit, a delight. I have one or two with me tonight. They would like to do something mischievous with your bucket (we'd had a leak in the roof).

Ada then talked about when she'd visited Eileen and Paul in their former home (as a spirit) and described things that had gone on, long before Paul's mediumship had started. Someone commented:

So the link was there even then?
Oh yes. You know, the links do not weaken, even though we have gone on our way. You have links with many. You would be surprised at just how many links you have with people in spirit. Yes, indeed.
Were you surprised when you passed?
I didn't think about it very much. I just enjoyed life. I was so absorbed in life when I was on your plane. I was not much interested in what came afterwards. So it was a nice surprise. I was very worldly in some ways. But I don't mean that in the way of possessions, but I was very absorbed in the every day world.
So do you mean you liked a chat and to know what was going on?
Yes, to be with people and enjoy people.
Did you believe in spirit when you were on the earth plane?
Only a little 'tot' every now and then. (Laughter). You really need to record all these jokes you know.

Shortly after this Ada said goodbye and left.

Chapter 24

Carol

Carol's Message:
Your Spirit Group are always connected to you

Carol is one of the original members of the Phoenix group. She has come through and chatted to us on a number of occasions; however, Hai has indicated that she is happy to stay in the background and that is why we don't get the opportunity to speak to her very often. We hadn't spoken to Carol for quite some time and one night a group member asked Hai whether she was still a member of the Spirit Group. He replied:

> Yes she is very near.
> *I thought she was always near.*
> She is, but she is nearer tonight.

Hai quickly left and Carol came through. George was intrigued and asked:

> *Carol, where are you when you are not near?*

Carol decided to tease and responded:
> A little further away.
> *I assumed that when the Phoenix group met, you were all in close proximity.*
> Yes indeed and we are all duly present.
> *Are you not allowed the odd Friday night off?*
> No, we are linked. We are linked to you and each other. Though we are not all actively present we are all connectedly present.

So you could still be doing other things but remain linked to us and know what was going on?
We are aware of what is going on.
Have you been somewhere else recently?

Carol replied:
The fisherman. (She was referring to the fact that George often fishes for information) I was in conversation with someone on a recent occasion but I simultaneously also knew exactly what was going on here. It is like; I can be having a conversation with someone but then can say; "Ah George has just said this, someone else has said that; they are doing this now or they are doing that now. They have recognised someone, they have sensed an energy change," and so on.
Do you sense that or—?
I connect with it. I *am* connected with it. It is like as if I had a television next to me and I could see everything you were doing, but it is closer than that. It is more connected than that.
Does that connectedness exist just on the nights we sit, or is it at other times as well?
I may connect at other times but it is a special occasion when you come together, and therefore, it is a special occasion when I connect to you.
So this idea we have, that you all come together as a group, is not necessarily correct, then. You could be anywhere doing anything but because of the connectedness you are here?
We are *here*, assuredly because of the connectedness. We are here as much as if we are here with you. We are very much still part of the group and are bound together as a group and the closeness of a group.
What would happen if you wanted to pursue another interest, would the group have to allow you to go?
(With amusement) The committee would review the situation.

This brought about some laughter. The reference to the committee was in relation to a conversation we'd had before going into the room to sit. Carol went on to tell us a little about her interests in the spirit world and finished by saying:

I fear we must draw this conversation to a close for tonight for the arts beckon. I have been most entertained and I have enjoyed myself wondrously so. I thank you for your conversation and for your company.

Chapter 25

Joseph

The Message:
Please communicate with us; we love it

Some of our 'Guest Speaker' spirits have indicated that communicating through our mediums on the earth plane is of particular interest to them. Joseph was one such spirit. He talked to us about the benefits of communication with the spirit world and encouraged us to keep trying even when things seemed difficult. Joseph also talked to us about some of the mechanics of communication and why it sometimes seems to go wrong. Joseph began the conversation by saying:

It is nice to be talking to you in your earthly abode.
Have you talked via a trance medium before?
No not like this. I have communicated with those who reside on the earthly plane in other ways, but not quite like this. I have usually imprinted my thoughts upon their minds.
Have you had any success?
Oh yes I have had success in conveying my impressions, which they kindly passed on.
Do you have a particular interest in communicating with people on the earth plane?
I just wish to do it because it's such a waste not to do it. Do you agree? If we can do it, why should we not do it, because when we do we participate in each other's company rather than being in 'separate rooms' with no means of communication. So it seems a pity that others do not try it more often. But of course they say to themselves; that cannot be right or that cannot be real, and so they don't try. But I would

put the question; if you do not try how can you know one way or the other. Is this not reasonable my friends? I admit that it is difficult. I admit that it is confusing even, at times, but I assure you that we *are* trying to reach to you from our side and when you are kind enough to try to reach to us from your side we have some success, some possibility of communication. Whereas, if you do not try to reach to us at all we could (smiling) grow very long arms, to no avail whatsoever.

Do you work with other spirits and give messages from them?

Well they are quite capable often of giving their own messages. They do not have particular need of me or others necessarily though there are some who are more experienced in this art. So, assuredly they give of their experience and benefit to those souls who are embarking upon the enterprise, to assist them in order to develop their skill, in a similar way that Isleen (spirit guide) helps you when you meditate. Therefore, out of comradeship, we try to develop the skills of others who are trying to reach you.

Do you have a particular link with the medium you work with?

At the time we do, because we establish a link, but it is like a flash of lightning almost, because you just connect, like the lightning connects the sky to the earth, and for as long as we are able to hold, each with the other, then the lightning perseveres and we are able to communicate. However, we can personally connect much easier with some mediums than is the case with others. So it is more like, the lightning is intermittent in some cases. It's on and it's off and it's on and it's off; you understand? So it is more difficult. Whereas, when we have a good strong communication, it is like; the lightning is permanently there for the duration of the communication. This is why when you have a medium conveying a message, if they are working with a connection which is more like intermittent lightning, it can become a little disjointed and vague at times. This happens because the message is on and off, broken up sort of thing, and therefore, it is more difficult. There is not the flow.

Do you sometimes give the medium a personal message, when you communicate?

Well we can do this but it's not so easy as to convey a message for someone else, a third party, because the medium, you see, is in *active* mode. They are expecting and anticipating a message to give to someone else and not a message to receive for themselves. However, when they are in their own stillness, it is true that we may convey a message to them for their own benefit because they are then more receptive to a message for themselves when they are in this state. You see, this state prompts and brings about different kinds of activity, different kinds of communication and messages.

Do you act as a spirit guide?

Well I do, at times, serve the purpose of a spirit guide but then who is a guide? Your dearest friend can be a guide to you on the earthly plane if they offer you some good advice or they ask you some sensible questions that get you to reflect upon your condition and circumstances. Is this then not acting as a guide? And so it is with us, who, as you say, act as guides from the spirit land. It is not that we act as guides as such; it is just that we ask you the right questions so that you can act as your own guide. This is the best way, the right way and so we just, sort of, provide some pointers, some indications, and some thoughtful reflections for you perhaps.

So presumably you know quite a bit about the medium that you're communicating with?

Yes sometimes, but at other times it is opportunistic. It is like; we throw out the bait and we get a snap and we take it up. We take the chance, the opportunity. So sometimes this is not so successful as it might be with someone whom we are familiar with. Sometimes it is remarkably successful because by chance, or whatever you wish to call it, there is a good rapport between us, and the medium concerned. So we have a varying state of affairs here but of course if we are working with someone we have been used to working with a good deal of the time and have grown accustomed to, and they to us, then the whole operation is much smoother, much easier, and much more predictable. It's like; if you had an old rickety car and you had difficulty in getting it into gear all the time, you wouldn't want to go out in it very often would you.

Joseph smiled and continued:

It is the same if we find a 'rickety' old medium with poor 'hearing' but the 'condition' of course is not peculiar to them, it is more the relationship between us that is the problem. It might be that we are not ideally disposed or connected to each other, and therefore, it feels like the gears are difficult to get into place.

So if you wanted to give a medium a message to give someone else, you would need to know the recipient quite well in order to give them a message that would be of benefit to them, would you?

Yes, to give them a clear message, but if we didn't know the recipient we could still perhaps convey something of use to them. It is a matter of relativity sometimes. We can convey something, which is of value, of use, but not to the depth and extent that could be possible under other circumstances.

Joseph decided it was time to finish the communication and finished with:

So it is time for me to say goodbye. I wish you luck in your endeavours.

Part 5

The Development of Trance Mediumship

Chapter 26

The Process

One member of our group was developing trance and the following communication took place in the early days of his development when it was difficult for his guide to talk through him. Our spirit scientist, WB, was asked a number of questions about the process.

I take it that the guide will eventually be able to access the speaking part of his brain?
Yes, there is no difficulty with that but it is finding the right *blending* in order for it to happen.
Can you explain how this blending occurs?
We reach towards you. It is a *bridging* and a *linking*, a *blending* of the spiritual and the physical and we have the ability to influence the physical mind; and therefore, the body, vocal chords and so on. It is like making a connection. It is like you with your electrical equipment; you plug in and the thing works and it is just like that with us. We come along with our lead and socket, we plug in and we are able to influence what occurs; but we've got to get the right fit. If we do not come with the right fit we are not able to achieve a smooth congruence, a good fit, then things do not go well. So this is the crucial thing; we must achieve a good match, a good fit.
Does all of this occur through the aura or is it on a direct physical level?
It occurs through a linking of the **spiritual** body of the medium, and this is linked to the **physical**. So, we link to the spiritual, and with that link, we also link to the physical.
So is it like a chain of events?

It is a chain and to talk of taking control or possession of the physical body is a misunderstanding. It is rather more interactive than that.

Doubts & Evidence

In the early days of communication with spirit, doubts and uncertainty are normal and there is a strong desire for hard evidence that the communication is indeed from spirit and not the result of an overactive imagination. Below is a conversation between Eileen and Hai about Paul's feelings and uncertainty about the process. We thought that by printing it here, it could help others in a similar situation.

Hai began by commenting:

> He (Paul) is troubled by uncertainty, but certainty *will* come.
> *Will Chung Ching,* (a guide who was communicating through another member of the group) *be able to provide evidence for Paul?*
> It will not happen in this way. It will happen in other ways, as evidence builds and as the phenomena develops. It is the very problem of the nature of our worlds, the very problem of the essence of life across all worlds. We are linked and interlinked and it is more difficult to prove the separateness and the individual existence of beings and minds because of our links; we are not separate. This makes proving things more difficult than if it was otherwise.

Sometimes when loved ones communicate, they are not always able to provide specific details of their life on the earth plane. They often give the impression that they cannot remember. Eileen was puzzled why they didn't check some facts before communicating and asked Hai:

> *When loved ones come, it's a pity they don't always understand how important it is to us, for them to bring evidence.*
> They understand but they must have free-flow; free-flow is hard to achieve.
> *Is it easier to achieve through mental mediumship?*

There is sometimes the illusion of more evidence through mental mediumship (clairvoyance) but it is no easier to provide concrete evidence.

People in this day and age want hard and fast evidence for everything.

They do want hard and fast evidence, as you say, though it is not the nature of life, of existence, to have this hard and fast evidence because the true evidence lies within. True evidence lies in reversing your insight, your perception, to discover your Eternal Source. This is the true evidence.

George Chapman, (healer) says in his book, that people who had met his spirit guide, (known as Dr Lang) before his death, were certain that it was indeed him who was working through the medium. So presumably the guide must have been able to provide a fair bit of evidence about himself?

Yes, so it may be sometimes that we are able to provide direct evidence from our historical lives because there is a flow, a bond, a communication to facilitate the memory and the recovery of facts.

The communication so far, has it been accurate or has there been anything that comes from Paul that is inaccurate?

The key turns the lock and it will turn more easily with time. What comes through is accurate in essence. We would wish to communicate more detail but this will take time.

The other things you wish to say, do you hold back because you think they will not come out as you intend?

No, not necessarily because it is the *detail* of evidence that we are working towards.

Trust

On another occasion someone asked, whether, in order to completely *let go* for trance, it was important to have complete trust in your Spirit Group. Hai replied:

It is true, it is developing a trust in us and in our work; this is true. And even though you trust us, even though you feel happy with us and are comfortable in our control, it is one thing to feel this, it is another thing to ask one of you, like Paul, to totally give himself up to us and to trust us when he is totally unconscious and has no control over what we say or do.

Is this largely what accounts for the drifting in and out during trance?
It is partly, because as the medium works with us or other spirits, they lapse into a comfort zone, if you like; relax into a state of relaxation and peacefulness and this enables them to drift more deeply. Providing they trust the experience, and they trust us, they will drift more deeply into our hold, into the state from which we may conduct things more directly, more deeply to advantage.

Working towards Trance

We thought the following would be especially useful to anyone who is either considering or developing trance mediumship. The questions relate to a particular member of our group who was developing trance mediumship.

Is the development of trance a long job then, Hai?
It can be, it is variable depending upon the state of development, upon the rate of progress, the opportunity to practise and so on.
Do you need to practise?
You need to *attune*, and if you do not make it too complicated, this practice is easily achieved.
Are these sensations that George is experiencing in his throat, the beginning of control?
It is the beginning of our ability to use the vocal chords, to express ourselves through the medium.

The 'Trainee' commented:

I seemed to go deeper than usual last week, Hai.
It is **letting go** that is the most difficult thing.
The spirit seemed to come in quite easily.
It is not just the coming in. You need to continue to **let go** even when the voice speaks, when the talking starts; this is the most difficult. When the voice is engaged and the speaking starts the mind may also engage, monitoring and commenting and internally discussing what it hears, and therefore, this is a problem to the medium. It is by letting go of all these activities that may lead to

greater fluency, which may lead to deeper trance and to deeper evidence. But, as you say, this is no easy matter.

Will I be completely knocked out?

You will be out sometimes but not all the time and not every time. The depth of trance may vary, and will vary for those also who are very experienced and for those who can attain the unconscious state.

Well I was partly aware at first, then went out and drifted back in again towards the end.

Yes this is how it often is.

Is that a good sign, when this drifting in and out starts, Hai?

Yes, it is indeed. It is a sign of development and it is a good sign but it all takes time and much patience, much giving up of effort also. This I know sounds a paradox but it is true; it is much—giving up of effort.

Is my forte trance mediumship, Hai?

You have opportunity, you have purpose, you have the possibility of developing your trance mediumship in the way you are doing now, so therefore, this is very possible. You could do with finding, George, further opportunities to practise beyond these nights, with your mediumship. We know this is not easy at present but in future more opportunities may arise. We have been able to 'fast track' you, to an extent, because you have had the potential and we were able to tap into that potential. By joining with us on these nights you have found that the energies have become accessible to you, and therefore, joining with this enterprise has assisted you in developing your gift.

You advised me not to practise on my own in the past. Has this changed?

We would advise you not to practise on your own for a number of reasons. Firstly, it is potentially dangerous if you were to go deeper and you went into the trance state without someone to monitor you. Nine times out of ten there would not be a problem. One time out of ten perhaps there would be one, and this is why we say you should not practise on your own.

Secondly, if you practise on your own there will be a tendency to monitor your own proceedings. This would create a barrier for you for your mind would begin to monitor too closely. You need to be in a situation where you can freely let go and allow someone else to monitor events for you. This helps the mind to still itself and to put itself at ease. It is then more able, to let go and give way to us, that we may enter and talk freely using the mind.

This is the way it is with Eileen and Paul. Eileen plays an important role in monitoring what goes on, in monitoring activity and fundamentally taking responsibility for having control of events. Some may think; "ah these spirits are able to talk through this person so they are in charge, they are in control, and we must do everything they say." **This should not be.** *You* must keep control of your side of life. *You* must have direction from your side of life—for it is *your* side of life, which *we* are invading and impress ourselves upon. **So it is your side of life, which has the authority of control in these situations and this is how it must be.**

Are there any exercises I could do on my own?

You may attune to us and to your spirit guides and by this attunement you will help the process naturally and you may feel spirits, without entering a deep trance state. This process, this regular practice of attunement, of feeling the energy without going into trance, is helpful and is a way of developing the connection. You may also find that you are given more images; you are given clairvoyant images, when you make such connections.

Do you make this connection through meditation?

We sometimes make the connection through meditation but it is more a process of *attunement*. You may attune to us; you may attune to other spirits and experience their energy and their power, without it being a meditative process as such; in the sense in which you are used to meditations.

An Experiment

Over the following months our Spirit Group tried a variety of ways to assist in George's development. One night we were sitting in the dark; it was our physical phenomena evening, and it is usual for Hai to open the proceedings by communicating through Paul. However, on this particular night, instead of Hai communicating through Paul in the usual way, he communicated instead through our developing medium. Hai explained that he had wanted to experiment, to help George to 'let go,' and so aid his development. A member of the group asked later:

Will you work with George again?

Yes, but for the moment we have to prioritise what we are about on these nights that you use for the development of physical phenomena. We cannot focus on two things at once so we perhaps need to focus a little more on George's development before we move on to physical phenomena again, but we should still sit as we sit.

Should we continue to sit in the dark?

Yes for who knows what we may accomplish.

Keeping the Development of Different Forms of Mediumship Separate

As stated above Hai has always said that during our physical phenomena sittings we should concentrate only on physical phenomena and that no attempt should be made for any other development on those nights. He has said that if a clairvoyant message or image comes naturally, or if someone spontaneously goes into trance, then that is ok. However, we should not *try* for it to happen during these sittings because it is important that we keep focus on what we are aiming to achieve. This seems to apply for all mediumship whether it is clairvoyance or trance; apparently it is not desirable to mix the two.

The conversation below shows how Hai re-emphasised this when a new member of the group asked if it was possible to develop trance during our physical phenomena sitting. Hai responded:

We have suggested that the development of trance is done on another occasion for we must focus our energies on the physical phenomena during these sittings. We work with you; we develop the energies and in developing the energies there will be, what you would call, 'spin off' for you, because, in developing the energies and in working with us, you attune yourselves more deeply to us. Therefore, by working with us, you will develop your faculties, almost incidentally. However, this is one thing, to develop the faculties incidentally, in passing, as we work with you, but there is a need on other occasions to be more focused with your development and to develop in specialised ways at these times. These different situations in which we work with you, can however, complement each other in moving us all forward, in developing our various abilities.

So, for those who are interested, can trance be developed on other nights?

It will depend upon what you wish, what focus you want. It is not possible to combine different activities on the same night unless you were to divide the night up for these specialised events, but you must then take account of your time and whether your time will allow this. Therefore, you must choose your priorities, you must choose what you wish to do, how you wish to spend the time, how you wish to develop. This is what *you* must decide.

Would it be useful if someone else developed trance for our physical phenomena sittings?

This would not be particularly helpful to these nights.

What about other nights, Hai?

Well it would be a case of developing the gift, the faculty, and seeing what comes. What I would say is that generally the development of trance takes much time, much effort and much patience. Therefore, it is perfectly possible, but you would need, ideally, to sit on other occasions, apart from the times that we guide you in.

Would there be any point in all of us developing it?

There would not be a lot of point; unless you were prepared to go your separate ways and set up your own groups that you may reach out to others. You are complementing each other well at the present time, but you must make your own decisions. We do not wish to straightjacket anyone.

At times there can be benefits to having two trance mediums in groups such as yours. It is also useful for other people to be present who have other specialised abilities and faculties. You, David, are gifted clairvoyantly and this complements nicely with what goes on in terms of our communication with you. You are also able to pick up changes in energy. This is useful because you can report this back to the group and this gives the group evidence, albeit of a clairvoyant kind, that things are developing and that something is going on.

Eileen is gifted with her healing and this is useful as a healing energy for the group because we are able to blend these different energies together to work to good effect. You also have need of people to *give* energy and to act as powerhouses for the group. We can then draw upon their energy, to good effect, to produce physical phenomena.

So you see, it is teamwork at the end of the day; and, it is only by teamwork, that we can achieve the purposes for which we all work. *You* must be a team, *we* must be a team, and together we must be a grand team.

Eileen referred to her guide and told Hai:

When Red Cloud last came to talk to us, I asked him about trance mediumship for healing but he wasn't too impressed. He said some mediums are good, others not so good.

If you have a specialised gift of healing this is important and should be pursued in its own right, for its own value, for its own power. If you are gifted to act as a trance medium in healing, then this should be pursued for the benefits that may accrue from it. However, if you do not have a gift for trance medium healing, then there is no point in using your energies in trying to develop it, because by devoting your energies to something that is not your forte you may undermine the powerful valuable gift that you do have.

How do we know whether we have a gift for a particular kind of mediumship?

You know by your intuition. You know by trying things out.

The conversation moved on and a question was asked about some changes noticed in Paul's face when he's in trance.

I've noticed that Paul's face seems to change when he's in trance. Is this ectoplasm or am I seeing this clairvoyantly?

A number of things may be happening, David. Sometimes his face may contort because of the pull of the energy in his facial muscles. This may be purely down to the contortions of the facial muscles. This is not as severe as in the early days, for we have refined the process of blending. However, they may contort, pull, and stretch, and this, in part, is to convey the mannerism or to achieve the tone of voice or manner that we wish to portray.

Sometimes you may also gain an impression of *our* spirit as we work through him; you may 'see' our spirit. Sometimes it may be clairvoyantly as you connect with our spirit and see us and at other times you may see us in your inner mind as you have done in the past.

Often we give Paul (the medium) an image of someone in the spirit world and then some of you will see the same image simultaneously. When you see us like a film in front of his face we may be trying to use a transfiguration approach to convey an image facially to you. So you will find varied conditions, varied manifestations of our energies.

A Spirits Experience

One night a new spirit was communicating with us and commented that he was feeling hot. A member of the group later asked Hai about the spirit's comments. Hai replied:

It is the experience of the manifestation that sometimes causes us to feel hot or warmth. At other times we may feel cold. It can vary. It is the manifestation of the connection and is merely the condition that arises when there is a joining.

Chapter 27

Isleen

Speaking on the Difficulties of Trance Communication

The room where we sit is a converted loft space. It is a beautiful peaceful room, which overlooks several gardens, and from our window we can see the hills in the distance. In the early days of communication, on one particular warm summer night, we had the windows open to keep the room a little cooler. We could hear the children playing robustly in the gardens below and the traffic, which we could hear easily through the roof, was particularly noisy. Anyone reading this who has a loft conversion and who lives on a main road will know exactly what we mean. So, we were talking to Isleen about these distractions and asked how much it was likely to affect Paul (the medium) and our communication with the Spirit Group, that night. Isleen answered:

You know it is a delicate balance speaking through him, and whether there is physical distraction from your world, or whether there is distraction from his mind, both can be problematic; both can cause problems and hinder the communication. So it is a delicate balance, an equilibrium that we must strive for and which at times will be near perfect and at other times will be far from perfect. Nevertheless, we can still achieve much, even with such imperfection.

Isleen was asked:

When Paul can go out ninety-nine-percent of the time, will that still present the same problem?

Isleen smiled and replied:

When we can achieve a greater 'knocking out' then the influences from his mind will be lessened and indeed this will help the process. But there can always be influences that interfere with the process. Loud noises from your side will interfere and even when in a more deeply unconscious state thoughts and images from his unconscious, which well up in the mind, may cause problems and distractions. So you see, it can never be an ideal process. Nevertheless, in spite of the difficulties we can achieve much and this is the case with all such communication.

There are some though, who are not aware of the potential for influences from sources other than our own spirit communication. You understand? But it is better to be aware of the danger than to not recognise it. For you can use your own judgment to censor what you hear, to select what you hear, to make judgements about what you hear. This is as it should be, because we must always take responsibility for our own thoughts, for our own actions and our own decisions.

When you knock Paul out further, will he be able to think his own thoughts, or is it like being asleep?

He may think his own thoughts in parallel to our thoughts and processes. It is like two machines running alongside each other on independent tracks but from time to time the tracks may touch and influence each other. It's a bit like your train lines and your points. Two tracks running parallel, separated, but you may switch the point and join the tracks and then you switch them again and so it is a bit like that with this process of communication.

So he can jump in and out of what is going on?

It is not so much that he jumps in and out but that the processes *touch* for a moment, for we are using a common conduit within his mind, within his nervous system. It is a process of partnership. We are only able to use this conduit because he has permitted it.

If he really didn't want to do it, then could he block you?

Then we would not be talking to you.

It's a wonder it works at all then, with all those complications.

Complications yes, yet of a simplicity beyond simplicity. I talk in riddles like Hai now, but it is true, that fundamentally, it is a simple process but it does have its complications. And we must be glad of it from both our sides, from both our points of view, for we are as dependent upon it as you are in order for this communication to take place. But it is one more illustration of the Oneness of life and the Suchness of life because if there was not a Oneness and a Suchness within our life, such processes would not be possible.

Part 6

Physical Mediumship/Phenomena

Chapter 28

We were unsure whether to include the following section in a book on spiritual awareness and development. So Eileen decided to ask Hai. Below is what he said in answer:

*   *   *

We think that it is alright to give people an overview of the phenomena, an impression of what is involved, yes, but without devoting too much of the book to it.

Still unsure, Eileen responded:
Some people, although interested in general communication with the spirit world, are not always keen to get involved with physical phenomena; I was concerned that it might not be of interest to everyone.

Hai continued:
So it may be that some are not so interested, for it is hard to bring about; it requires much devotion and patience to bring about. There are those who are more interested in developing mediumship so they may give messages and they develop as an individual person, usually. Whereas, sitting for physical phenomena, is more of a *communal* thing. Not everyone is interested in this approach but it is the highest, in some ways, because it does rely, and rely very strongly upon the communion and the harmony between you.

*   *   *

How it all Started

So here it is—but before you read what the spirits have to say about our efforts at producing physical phenomena we thought we'd better fill you in with some of the background to how it all started.

We began sitting for physical phenomena during the latter part of 1999. Paul had become particularly interested in this aspect of mediumship having joined ASAP (Association for the study of Anomalous Phenomena.) However, to experiment for physical phenomena we needed more than the two of us. We knew several people from our local mediumship development group but quickly realised that most saw physical phenomena as something quite different and for some, even a little scary.

We were aware that it was possible to advertise for 'sitters;' however, neither of us were naturally extrovert by nature and so held back from taking this step. One day our regular quarterly journal from the Noah's Ark Society dropped through our door and we spotted an advertisement from a couple who wanted to join an *established* physical phenomena circle. The couple lived within an easy car ride but we were acutely aware that, because we had not actually *established* a circle, we did not fit their requirements. We put the journal aside and went off to take a few days break in London.

As a treat for our holiday we'd booked a private sitting with Elizabeth Hill, at the Spiritualist Association of Great Britain. That sitting filled us with even more enthusiasm to seek out physical evidence of survival so we came home with renewed energy to pursue our goal.

By now several weeks had passed since we'd spotted the advertisement and Eileen took the view that if the advertisers hadn't yet received any offers, then they might just be prepared to join us in setting up a circle of our own. We took the plunge, made the phone call and shortly after we held our first physical phenomena séance.

Our sessions took place regularly every Friday night. We did not have our loft conversion then, so we used the small dining room, which leads on to the kitchen in our home. The room has two doors to it (both glass) and a large bay window. It was impossible to black it out completely but we used pieces of thick black garden plastic to block out as much light as possible.

Those evenings were very enjoyable and lasted over a year. All four of us got on extremely well and quickly became good friends. We would sit in the dark listening to classical music (and some not so classical) whilst, at the same time, noting any energy changes that took place. We'd not managed to achieve total blackness during the sessions; nevertheless, at different times, two of us received a strong tug to our clothing and another felt a definite tap on the knee. Eventually, due to a change in their personal circumstances, our friends were unable to continue with our sittings. By this time we'd had our loft converted. We'd also met others who were interested in joining our sessions.

There followed many changes within the group membership. This is inevitable with any group of people who meet regularly. However, when the expectation is for weekly attendance, apart from holidays and sickness, there is bound to be a higher dropout rate. We are now a group of five and have been together for some years.

We are able to 'black out' our room completely from external light to conserve energy and we've experimented with a 'cabinet' for Paul, and a 'glass dome.' We also have other 'tools' around for the Spirit Group to have a go at moving. These include a plywood cone (also known as a trumpet) bells, marbles, pen, paper and crystals. The cabinet and the glass dome will explained further as you read the following chapters.

We've received taps and tugs at our clothes and our CD is now being turned off on a regular basis. It's always at a different point on the disc and the way they do it seems to vary. Nevertheless, I think even the Spirit Group would agree, the phenomena is still spasmodic. We are told that they need to get the 'consistency' right and when they do they will be able to reproduce effects on a regular basis. In the meantime we will continue to sit each week, sing along to the music and thoroughly enjoy each other's company.

*   *   *

Questions on Physical Mediumship/Phenomena

Use of the sitters Energy

Hai was asked:

When sitting for Physical phenomena, is it better that we are all healthy or does it make no difference?

We may draw on each of you, according to your capacity, according to your need.

So if we were all very fit and healthy would you be able to draw more?

We may be able to draw more but we can also draw our energies from other energy fields, such as your earth, or from a spiritual dimension or the energies from your atmosphere.

*   *   *

Traditional v Modern

I read a book where spirit children were able to open Christmas presents that had been left out for them. Would this have been possible?

Yes this is possible.

Why is this phenomena not produced nowadays?

It is produced nowadays, but rarely so, because people do not sit, people do not persevere with the attempt; people do not put the time in. There are so many distractions in your world, so many enticing sweets to unravel.

The same book said, the medium was awake and was able to watch the children opening the presents. How could this have happened?

The medium may, under certain circumstances, become conscious and participate in the seeing of the physical. There is no difficulty with this when conditions are right.

Is the spirit world still happy to work with that sort of phenomena?

We are.

I wondered whether there was a shift towards computer evidence these days.

We may use a variety of techniques to make contact with people. Using modern machinery to make contact is one way, but there is a place for traditional methods also.

Movement of Objects in the Home

Hai was asked:

Can spirit move things in our homes?

Yes they can but those near your realms do so more easily. On our levels it is not so easy unless we have a helper.

Does it have to be a loved one?

It can be done by anyone. It does not necessarily have to be a loved one but a loved one may do so to try to attract your attention, to make you aware of their presence, yes.

Why is it easier if they are nearer to the earth plane?

They are nearer your vibration and can influence your vibrational energies more easily than we can on the more refined energy levels.

Are they spirits who have not been passed over very long?

Passed over in some sense, but left here.

You mean they are too close to earth?

Yes, too close to earth, too attached to earth. They need to float up (laughs.)

So, if a spirit has actually arrived in their proper place in the spirit world but came back to visit a loved one, would they still be able to manipulate the energies, or does that apply only to someone who hasn't actually moved into the spirit world yet?

It depends on the vibrational energy as to what they may achieve but they may be able to influence physical things of your earth if they are not too far removed from the vibrations. It becomes more difficult when they move to other realms.

In her book, Gay Muir, talks of people who've lost loved ones, having keys moved around etc. Is the discarnate spirit using the energy of the loved one, to be able to move these objects?

They are able to blend their own energies with the physical energies of the earth, of other people, and so accomplish some of these things.

It seems strange to me that we sit here every week and can only achieve a very small amount of phenomena. Do the people concerned have more energy than us?

No. It is a knack; it is fortuitous circumstances coming together.

Direct Voice

On another night WB was asked what direct voice was and how it was achieved. He replied:

It is achieved by a couple of different approaches. One approach uses the ectoplasm from the medium and from the sitters to form an energy box, through which we, as spirits, may project ourselves directly. So, instead of using the voice box of the medium, as I am doing now, we can use the voice box, which is made of ectoplasm, or some other form of specialist energy. Therefore, it is more direct, more immediate, but the voice box is still attached to you, as sitters, and the medium in particular. Therefore, it may still be influenced by the unconscious mind of the medium but it is a more direct route and a more direct expression as is possible.

Chapter 29

Tools to help Physical Phenomena

Preparing the Room

Hai was asked:

Is it better that a room used for physical phenomena, is not used for anything else?

Well, it is sometimes the case, but we know it is difficult to achieve these circumstances. But it is not too essential, for we know of many instances where rooms have been used for different purposes and yet physical phenomena are achieved. Therefore it is not essential; but it is helpful to have spiritual focus; focus for spiritual energies, spiritual work, rather than use the room for all kinds of things. You see, even when you do your meditations and have your other sittings, you build up energies in this room and these energies all help to build up the potential for physical phenomena.

I was aware that many mediums have achieved physical phenomena in rooms that are used for other purposes but I thought that the reason might be that they are extremely powerful mediums.

It is true that if they are powerful physical mediums, they are less constrained by these factors, but it is still possible to achieve these things given the circumstances of your room.

Salt & Water

We'd been advised to put salt and water in the room, to aid physical phenomena. Hai was asked:

How does the salt and water work?

Salt and water are basic minerals of the earth, basic building blocks, basic ingredients of life. Therefore, they have a role to play in the primeval 'soup' of physical phenomena and ectoplasm.

Do we have enough in this room?

You have enough and more than you need.

Is there anything else we need?

Yes, commitment, determination, and patience, (laughs) which you have.

Music

Hai had suggested that if we played some music and sang along to it for ten minutes or so, it would help raise the energies. This we did with great gusto, though none of us would consider ourselves singers. This caused much amusement between our spirit friends and they would often comment, 'tongue in cheek,' on the great effort we put into our singing. Of course we also 'suffered' the obvious jokes about our singing too, from some of our, shall we say, less sensitive spirit friends. This, of course, is always done 'in the best of spirits' and the laughter that results from the jokes further aids the raising of the energies.

When Henry came one night the conversation inevitably got around to our singing. Henry lived his last earth life in America and in a southern accent he had the following comments to make:

The loving harmony, which you send out folks, is truly music to our ears. So don't you fret none about the quality of your tonal output (laughing) don't let them rib you too much about that 'cause they are all saying it with one big tongue in their cheek. Because, to be sure, it's like I say, a loving harmony singing out from you folk and—it is music to our ears. So bye folks I'll be seeing you. I'll be keeping an eye on you as well as chatting to all those folks up here. Goodbye to you.

*   *   *

Carol; member of the Phoenix group also commented upon our singing. She was asked:

What do you think of our group now then, Carol?

It is a nice group that you have gathered around you and we will work with this group diligently. There is a chink of light between the doors, which are opening. (This was meant symbolically) The light floods in and though you do not see it, the light does floods in and will flood in more as the doors open.
Oh, so there is a start then, is there?
There is a start, more than a start.
Does the singing help?
The singing helps because you are showing your harmonious togetherness, because you are displaying your commitment and generating energy. These things are worth doing so continue with your singing.

Glass Domes Cones and Cabinets

For a period we experimented along the lines suggested by the Scole Experimental Group, which relies on energy to produce phenomena rather than ectoplasm. In part this involved experimenting with a glass dome. The dome is placed on a table in the room during sittings and energies are stored in it to be used later by the Spirit Group as required.

We have also used a portable cabinet for Paul (the medium) to sit in during our physical phenomena sittings. We'd also acquired a plywood cone, sometimes known as a trumpet, which we'd affectionately named Rosie.

The following is a conversation with our Spirit Group about these experimental aids and it demonstrates the importance of recognising that each group will be composed of different energies, and therefore, different methods may well be required to obtain phenomena.

Domes

We'd been sitting for some time with the dome but hadn't noticed anything significant. Hai was asked:

Will we ever see any energy inside the dome?
It is possible; you may see lights inside the dome, which is the energy.
Are some groups having more luck with these domes?

Some are because the energies are just right. But we've concluded that sometimes one group is best working one way and another group another way. It is a matter of the blending of energies and sometimes the particular blending of energies does not favour this approach; it favours another approach. We suspect you would be better to remove the dome for a time and to proceed in the traditional way and see how we progress.

Cones *(Trumpet)*

Does it matter where we place (our cone) Rosie?
No it doesn't matter where Rosie is. You should have water in the room though as this helps to create the ectoplasm.
Why is Rosie different from the dome in terms of energy, Hai?
The purpose of the dome is to store energy. The purpose of Rosie is to respond to the energy.

Cabinet

WB was asked:
What purpose does a cabinet serve?
A cabinet serves to condense the energy prior to its release into the environment and it's focusing on the object, which we are attempting to move in some way or other.
Do all our energies channel into Paul?
For the purposes of some physical phenomena the energies are drawn and focused, if you like, through a particular person. It is like a funnel or a magnifying glass or something of that nature. We need all your energies but we need them focusing in a certain way.
Would the energies automatically be enhanced in a cabinet?
We work with the energies in drawing upon them and in focusing them. The cabinet merely assists us with this process. The process is not particularly different; it is merely a tool to further enhance our activity and our efforts.
Does the cabinet have to have a lid on it?
It does not need a lid necessarily, but the more it is contained the better.
What about a curtain rail on the ceiling, will that do?
This will do admirably, yes.

Ectoplasm

Someone had been reading an article on ectoplasm and asked WB:

Would it be possible for someone to take a sample of ectoplasm without hurting the medium or the other people present in the room?
A small piece would not be detrimental but it is most unusual to be able to do this because ectoplasm is of an intermediary nature between your plane and the spiritual plane. It does not fit directly into either because, in a sense, it is intermediary.

Red Lights and their Significance in the Physical Phenomena Setting

Why is a red light important at a sitting, but not other colours?
The red light—this aspect of white light, does not destroy the ectoplasm and it is a subdued light. It facilitates the development of physical phenomena and does not obstruct it.

Spirit Influence on Magnetic Tapes

When typing up one of our recorded meditations, Eileen noticed a noise that had not been observed during a meditation. She asked Hai about this:

He told us:
It is possible for us to influence the magnetic tapes, (he uses the word tapes because Eileen had inadvertently used that word instead of mini disc) and other various kinds, to imprint an image or sound by using our energies. This will impact upon the tape to produce an effect that you may hear and recognise. At times we may accomplish a physical sound that you may hear with your physical ear and which will be recorded upon the tape. However, at other times, we may be able to use our energies to register a sound upon a tape that you have **not** heard with your physical ear until you play back the tape. We must be versatile in using what is available to us. What is sound—but energy. And we may use our energy to create sound even if you cannot hear the sound in your room.

Filming the proceeds

A new member of the group showed us some film where he had managed to pick up orbs and other interesting things. Paul decided he would like to try this during our sittings for physical phenomena so we bought a camcorder with infrared light so that it could be used in the dark. Below are some of the questions our group asked Hai resulting from this experiment.

Eileen commented:

Paul was saying that the camera last week revealed a bright flash of light, Hai.
Oh yes. We have been busy you see, creating your phenomena which you seek.
Was it pure energy or something else?
Ah yes, this is energy, which we are able to manipulate to create light.
It was very quick.
Well you know we have to work very hard to create a little bit of phenomena. So though you only see it in a 'twinkling of an eye' it requires much effort on our part.
Once you are able to generate something like that, does it become easier to repeat the exercise?

Smiling Hai replied:
Ah yes, instead of lasting for a twinkling of an eye it will last for two twinklings of the eye. This is great progress.
Are the orbs of light we find on the camcorder film, beings of some kind, or is it simply, energy that is showing up on the film?
They may have different sources. They may reflect energies that we use when we are in your world. They may also reflect ourselves in a more essential way because we too may be picked up, at times, as orbs of light. However, your small orbs are usually to do with our *manifestations* rather than *us*, if you follow me.
Would there be others also that wouldn't necessarily show up on the cameras?
Your instruments pick up in certain ways. They pick up vibrations, they pick up frequencies, but each of your instruments is limited by the

frequencies it can pick up. You may well, in the future, develop new instruments that will have a greater range or a more specific range, which will then be able to pick up more manifestations of spirit. We talk of spirit and we talk of the material world but in reality they are *one,* as you know, so there is not this division of a spiritual material really. We exist on different dimensions; different vibrations and frequencies but the One Reality pervades all.

Orbs

On another night Hai was asked questions along a similar theme.

A friend of mine has been picking up orbs on his camera. Can you explain what they are?

Hai asked where the orbs had been detected and replied:

Well he is picking up aspects of spiritual energy. These sometimes are a semblance of spirit folk but other times are a semblance of energies *produced* by spirit folk, so they are not necessarily spirits themselves you see, but they may be energies associated with spirits. So either way he is picking up something of interest, some spiritual energy, yes.
What do you mean when you say the orbs are a semblance of spirit folk rather than you (spirits)?
They are a *signature* of us, the energy signature of us, a manifestation of us, not so much us ourselves.
Almost like your aura or something like that?
Not even as direct as that, more like the effects of the aura on the environment.
Like a footprint in the ground?
Just so.
So it wouldn't mean that the spirits were actually in the room then?
Yes it will mean there *are* spirits in the room but the orbs are not the spirits, nor are they a direct manifestation, but rather a subtle extraneous manifestation.
So the orbs occur because there is a spirit moving around, but are not the actual spirit, is that right?

Yes.

One member of the group, George, changed the questioning slightly. He asked:

Do ley lines have any affects on these occurrences?
It may sometimes, George. It may have bearing upon what is caught on the camera, yes. Sometimes ley lines can facilitate, can help to generate these orbs. There are many different types of orb, you understand. Some are produced by the earth's magnetic field, by the energies of the earth. But those of which you speak are most likely generated by spiritual forces.

*   *   *

One night the group were discussing how the camera had picked up some orbs of light the previous week. Hai commented:

Yes we managed to generate some lights.
Is that the start of the phenomena then, Hai or do they occur naturally all the time.
We generate them. So we are generating something new for you. You may find other kinds of lights that are to do with lights of the earth but these were not they.
So if we just left the camera running in this room but you were not generating the lights, then it wouldn't record anything?
Well you can try that experiment.

One member of the group commented that he thought he'd seen an orb in his office that day. Hai replied:

Yes you may pick it up with your eyes from time to time if conditions are right. It is most likely when you are simply going about your business, and by accident almost, it will seem to happen.

Chapter 30

WB
Spirit Scientist

In this chapter you will find some of the communications we received from our spirit scientist, WB. In the early days WB would regularly come through to talk to us about our progress with our physical phenomena sittings and at the same time offer encouragement with our efforts. Some of WB's communications can sound quite formal; however, there are times when his 'lighter' side is more in evidence. We wanted to give the reader a full picture of WB so, in the transcripts below, you will find snippets that are not necessarily related to physical phenomena but do, however, offer a more rounded picture of his personality.

*   *   *

One night WB was asked whether there was anything more we could do to assist in the proceedings. He told us:

Try to do your bit to achieve the harmony. You should try and keep things jolly, happy, light—not serious. Beyond that, it is up to us. There is enough energy here; it is a matter of coordinating the energy, pulling it together.
Does the energy remain in the room until next week?
There is some residue but it is not that important. As we all work together it becomes easier and more possible to 'kick start' the night, if you like. It is like; we can straight away plug in and switch on so we do not have to worry so much about preliminaries. We are able to link

together with you and 'kick start' the energy. There are times of course where you feel there is not much happening but I assure you there is.

We use the energy in different ways, in preparation; so we remain hopeful. In the meantime we arrange regular changing of the scenery (reference to the regular spirit visitors from different time periods) and you will find that there are some of the regulars, as you have become accustomed to and from time to time there will be some new persons making an appearance. This may be because *they* wish to make an appearance. At other times *we* have 'thrown them into the arena' because we have persuaded them that they have an important contribution to make and they have graciously acceded to our request.

*   *   *

We'd been experimenting with different music and taking turns to go quietly within. WB was asked:

Does our new system help, WB?
I think it is of merit, of interest to try this for some time. You must experiment from your side as we experiment from our side. We are all experimenters in this. There is no magic formula beyond the harmony, which you create. Raising the energies, of course, is a vital component and you are admirably employed by your musical accompaniments and your singing in order to raise these vibrations.

*   *   *

One night, a couple of members of our group had heard a buzzing noise during the session and George took the opportunity to ask WB about it.

He told us:
We were attempting to vibrate the air in some way to create a sound. It is not the easiest of things to do. It worked in small measure but it did not work so that you all could hear. You were not all close enough to it.

Eileen commented:
Probably our raucous singing prevented us from hearing.

Well we must have some raucous singing, as you say, to raise the energies in the first place. I would not criticise on that count.

*   *   *

On another occasion WB told us:

We have been trying to do something different tonight. Trying to move forward my friends in our joint endeavours.
Have you been successful?
We have had some measure of success in harnessing the energies but I fear we have not achieved our aim of harnessing and refocusing them to the desired degree; but we have made some progress we feel, yes. We are doing well if we can move forward on our journey of exploration, my friends. We would wish you to have more people go quietly within, periodically during the evening for a little time. You may take turns.
So, how many at a time?
Just a couple at a time, we would like to experiment with your energies. Ten to fifteen minuets each would be sufficient. We would like to try to harness different energies to experiment with the effect.

WB then went on to explain how they can assess and process our different energies when deciding upon which to use. Eileen asked if we had all been processed in this way.

Yes, (smiles) though we have not done you all tonight you understand.
Do you have a database then?
We can process the energies in different permutations to facilitate our enterprise. You need to become passive, to go with the flow.

*   *   *

On our physical phenomena nights it is usual for Paul, after we've finished talking to Hai, to come out of trance. Paul is then free to sing with the rest of us to raise the energies. On this particular night he'd remained in trance for some time after Hai left. When WB came through at the end of the session, Eileen commented:

I wondered whether you were taking Paul deeper tonight.

We were, we held onto him yes. We held on longer than has been the practice in the past. We will continue to hold onto him longer on other occasions in the future to try to take him deeper, (smiling) within our grip, in the nicest possible way.

Evidence

Another night WB talked to us about the need for evidence of the spirit world. He told us:

Even in my day there were colleagues around me who believed in certain theories and this was not always based on evidence. Evidence is crucial, is it not? We must proceed with our discoveries and explorations on the basis of our evidence otherwise we would just progress based on fancy, which is insecure ground. Therefore, evidence is vital. I have met many people, many great minds while I have been over here (spirit world.) I was impressed with Newton for his clear thinking approach.

Do the scientists carry on with the same type of work when in spirit?

Yes, but we do not have to. We are not committed to it by anybody else but we may choose to carry on with our enthusiasm, with our particular realm of discovery if we so wish. I have chosen this and I am now looking at the laws which link the physical and the spiritual, the underlying unity of energies between the spiritual and physical and this is what has drawn me to my work with Hai.

Is there a time difference between these energies?

Time is ultimately meaningless dear sir. Time is a construction without a central substance.

Do energies need to be changed to progress?

It is not a matter of *changing* energies as *recognising* them. It is a process of *recognition* that people become more aware of the links, the underlying unity between the spirit worlds and the earth planes. Your science will continue to develop and in time the barriers, which seem so substantial now, may start to fall away a little.

Are there spirit groups working like this in other countries?

Absolutely. We have groups working in all the worlds; not just this earth, this galaxy, but in all the galaxies.

Personal Evidence and WB's description of the Collection and Use of Energy

It is certainly true, that the best evidence is that which is personal to us. One night when the group were talking to WB, Eileen commented that during a previous sitting, Paul had felt a tug on his trouser leg. WB responded initially, by talking of the need for evidence. He then went on to describe, in the best way he could, just what happens when the Spirit Group collect and use energy for physical phenomena.

He told us:

Yes, we were successful (in tugging Paul's trouser leg.) It was unambiguous, it was clear, and this is how all physical phenomena must be. It may not be that you all experience the same thing at the same time. This is not feasible always. Nevertheless, if you individually experience something clear and unambiguous, this is a big step forward and this is what we would wish to happen because this will be the first development.

You will *individually* have separate experiences, but clear experiences just the same and you individually will be in no doubt of the experience and of the reality of your experience. However, if you tell your partner on the other side of the room, they might think; "oh Joan is a bit imaginative tonight;" but you will know yourself, Joan, and Paul also, was in no doubt about his experience; that it was unambiguous. So this is what we must hope for first, before we move forward, and when we do move forward we hope to create the experiences which you all may experience simultaneously; so we beaver away.

And you know it *is* like the beaver because the beaver has to level many trees to make the dam but until he puts all the little twigs in place, the water comes in quite significantly. Eventually he gets it just right, to perfection, and then you have a big lake form behind the dam. There are difficulties of course because we must create a big lake behind the dam. We must then quickly pull the plug out, because with the energy of the big lake, if we pull the plug out and we release that energy to create some physical phenomena, we've then got to put the plug back in and build the reservoir up again; that of course takes some time.

However, as we go on we will find that the reservoir will be replenished more quickly because the process has become more natural, more routine. Therefore, it becomes a quick and easier process and we may regenerate the lake more quickly, regularly pull out the plug and create all sorts of interesting effects.

Psychic Research Centres

WB was asked:
What does the spirit world think of these psychic research places we hear about?

You will as human beings wish to investigate in the hope of proving something, in the hope of gaining evidence. However, I fear that this, for the moment, is a very difficult enterprise to bring to a satisfactory conclusion. What is evidence for one person will not do as evidence for another and though some may feel they have achieved concrete evidence in their experiments and may feel that the evidence will do very well for those who are not present, there will always be the doubt about the validity of the evidence and the research. Therefore, for the time being, I think you are in a difficult situation as far as evidence goes.

Evidence and proof, I feel, are still a matter for the individual's investigation and satisfaction. You may gather your evidence and it is perhaps the accumulative nature of the evidence that will convince you, as fully as you can possibly be convinced in your present limitations, rather than the evidence of scientific experiments.

I always believe my messages and I find it difficult to understand why scientists don't believe too, if they receive convincing messages.

Scientists must be able to touch things. At the end of the day they are looking to be able to touch things, if not with their hands, then with their minds, with a *certainty* that goes beyond doubt. But we are not dealing here with a thing that can be easily measured which is what they are used to.

Even within your own earthly sciences, some of them are in their infancy and the hardliners would be reluctant to even acknowledge them to the scientific community. I speak of your psychologists and such like and the experiments, which these other sciences do. Likewise the hard-line scientists will shake their heads in dismay and say this proves nothing. How much more difficult is it with our enterprise, to provide scientific evidence in this form.

Introducing New Members into the Group

We asked WB whether we should allow other people to join us to allow for the times when regular members could not attend. His response was interesting:

> If you bring in new people it will take time before they become used to what is going on so you will take a step back; however, this can lead to you taking a step forward again later. You should view yourselves as scientific experimenters in all this, in the actual venture itself, and adopt an experimental attitude. This might help with some of your members who are over sceptical perhaps. You should give yourselves freely to the experiment without feeling a necessity to believe everything. We have to blend the energies, which you are not aware of normally in your day-to-day existences but these energies are there, locked within your physical bodies. The energies that are associated with ectoplasm are very subtle.

Consistency of Group Membership

We'd been sitting for well over a year and some members of the group were finding it difficult to keep up with the weekly sessions. Eileen asked:

> *If some members cannot come every week can their energy be stored and used on another night?*
>
> Yes, it is true that the energies may be stored. We do not use the energies always on the night; in fact we do not do this at all. We always leave some in reserve and we store the energy as best we might. And we do not have consistent gathering from our side either because they are taken away by various events, which requires their presence; nevertheless, this is not a serious hindrance to our enterprise. The key players are present; this is the most important thing.

One person, who could not be present every week, asked:

> *Does it help if I think of everyone when I can't be present?*
>
> It is helpful, Joan. I would not wish you to be sat in some chair for three hours sending benevolent thoughts to us, but if you can spare yourself for five

minutes or so and project your loving supportive thoughts to the venture, it is a big help because *you do connect* at a certain level.

Even when you are all separate you are not separate my friends, you must realise this. You are not separate from each other and you are not separate from us. A thread, if you wish to view it in this way, links us all, for there is no separateness, there is interconnectedness always. We are all linked together. So if you can send your loving thoughts it will be of benefit.

Always build in the *loving feeling*, the loving element, my friends, for this is were the power lies. In other words, it is not just in a visual thing, though the visual will help you to send your thoughts, but it is more effective to imagine the person *visually*, and at the same time, *feel* loving thoughts. This will be a boost, a help to them.

Do we have to send our loving thoughts to the spirits, or can it be to the members of the group?

No, you can simply think of this room, you can think of the people gathered here. It does not matter. In linking to the room, in linking to the people in this room, you also link to us for we are all gathered to meet and share together, and therefore, if you form a mental link to this room, you are linking to us also. So, it does not have to be a complicated art in mental gymnastics.

*   *   *

In all our investigations into physical phenomena and the books we've read about how to achieve it, the information has been consistent in that it always suggests that, to ensure consistency, all sitters should sit regularly. We'd had a few members of the group come and go over time, and we therefore, became concerned when another member's attendance became spasmodic. We wondered whether she really wanted to continue with the sessions and what, if any, difference her intermittent visits made on the proceedings. WB advised us on this:

Her heart is in the right place. You must just accept people for what they are, for what they give. The energies are good, as you have been told before; therefore, for as long as people wish to participate then you should gratefully accept. Just let things take their course.

So it's better that she comes sometimes than not at all?

Yes, you have formed a bond; a grouping, and therefore, you may use this. It is helpful and it works. But you will have to be patient with each other from time to time; it is the nature of things.

It's not been easy with all the coming and going of the various members.

Yes, this is very difficult; we realise this. There is no easy solution I fear, for it is the human earthly condition for there to be change, for people to move on and for new people to come, but while you can create or support some kind of consistency it is helpful.

Chapter 31

Jon

Jon's communication covered a wide range of topics but we have extracted here what he had to say about physical phenomena. We were not sitting for physical phenomena on this particular night so we had a low light on in the room.

Jon took some time in coming through and while this was happening someone in our group commented that the white light on the lamp was getting brighter. Others who were facing the lamp were able to confirm this. Jonathon did not speak for a while, preferring instead to hum a tune. He continued for a minute or so, then had the following comments to make about our lamp:

We are attempting to influence your environment, as far as we may in these conditions, for these conditions are not ideal conditions.
Did you alter the light?
We attempted to alter the light.

One member of the group referred to a shadow we'd noticed earlier and asked:

Did you cause the shadow?
Not directly but a shadow may have been your perception of what we tried to do.
What are, ideal conditions, for you to alter our environment?
Total blackness.
Is the light too bright for you?
It is damaging, harmful to the energies, so we try to influence your electronic devises to achieve some change in their energy level. There

is scope for playing around with your energy devises in order to achieve some impact upon them, some change of their condition; momentarily.
Have you got some particular experience of changing lights, etc?

Jon laughed and replied:

Oh yes, yes. I enjoy making lights go up and down.
Were you interested in this kind of thing when you were on the earth plane?

Jon was obviously feeling light-hearted and answered accordingly:

Oh yes, I like to have good lighting in the place.
So were you interested in the spirit world and physical phenomena?
No. Why bother with what you can't see?
Had you heard of physical phenomena?
I'd heard of it, from those who believed it.
But you didn't?
No.
Do you believe in it now? (Laughter)
I have been somewhat confounded in my attempt not to believe it, if you follow me.
So you've got your evidence from the spirit world?
I have, and I would be in somewhat of a predicament if I persevered and persisted in my belief that it does not exist, for I would have to come to the conclusion that this is the real world and you are a figment of my imagination, a spirit world which does not exist. Do you follow me?
In other words you can see us?
I can see you; I can hear you, loud and clear.
Do you visit other groups and play around with their lighting systems?
No, you are a one off, a specialty.
Why were you humming when you first came through?
I was singing something that I recollected because I connected with this physical body. It's funny you know, when we connect with the physical body; sometimes it awakens memories, which we do not particularly remember otherwise.

Chapter 32

Lennox

Lennox's Message:
Make sure you get the Music Right

Lennox came through one night when we were sitting for physical phenomena and, as explained in an earlier chapter, it is customary on these nights to sing along to a few lively songs, to help raise the energies. This particular night we were trying out a new CD that contained songs from the sixties. We were singing along to the music, when Lennox came through and joined in with the singing. He spoke with an American accent and told us he'd been a singer in the sixties, but apart from this we could not engage him in further conversation. He was clearly only interested in 'feeling' the beat of the song and singing along with us. This 'ritual' continued for several weeks. Lennox would come through at a certain point in the CD, sing along for three more tunes, and then disappear. Suddenly his visits stopped and we didn't hear from him again for some months.

We eventually got tired of that particular CD and began using another one, which did not include the songs that Lennox had enjoyed so much. One night one of our spirit visitors told us, that Lennox would come back and sing with us again, but we would need to record some of his favourite songs on our new CD. We agreed to do this but time went on and we never seemed to have time to do it. One night we received another visit from Lennox, this time without his favourite music to entice him. Below is what he told us:

They told me it is no use me expressing my wishes, my wants, from some other folk. I should come and explicitly express them to you, yeah. I've been told that if I want some bright music, I've got to come and speak to you folks and I've got to put in my special request, because it's going to put you folk to some trouble. So I have to put *myself* to some trouble; they say to me. So I'm wishing you to record on your new disc, one or two songs from that other disc that you used to play. For they tell me, that I could help with your energies; if you will kindly oblige me by allowing me to join you folks.

How can you help with the energies Lennox?

By singing along. The less kindly ones have suggested, (laughing) and this might be a ruse on their part, I suspect, but they have suggested that by contributing in this way I may help the beat and the tunefulness of your rendering. But you know, I have not said this. I am so mighty pleased to be able to join in with you all when I get the chance. (Laughing again) I'm oblivious to your singing anyway.

I will include your request on our next disc, Lennox.

Well I'll be mighty grateful.

We did record another CD, and included Lennox's favourite tunes, and for a while he returned to the group to sing along with us. We haven't heard from him for some time now so we think he may have joined another group. Perhaps the singing was better.

Chapter 33

Jonathan
The Scientist (and the Poet)

Jonathan was another Guest Speaker who had an interest in physical phenomena. Like WB, he too had been a scientist when last on the earth plane.

Jonathan was asked:
Are we doing all right with the physical phenomena?
Yes, you are doing excellently well on your part but we, on our part, must try harder. However, we are all doing well together and this is what we must do, work together. This is what we would expect and hope for.
Do you think we should sing less, and have a longer quiet time during the sessions?
No, not particularly, but you do not need to sing *all* the time. You may put the music lower and converse with each other if you wish.
It's difficult not to sing when the music is on.
We do not make any rules over this. Whatever you find conducive to your harmony.
Shall we just talk about every day things?
Yes, and not so every day things, also.
Can we do anything more to help?
You can help us by reaching out to us, by retaining the connection, by aiding the connection, but this is quite sufficient. You are all doing admirably well.
Could this take many, many years?

We would hope that we could generate something before then. But you know it is like building one foundation on top of another.

Eileen told Jon about a spirit scientist who'd visited the week before, and had managed to switch off our CD player by using the energies. When asked how he'd managed to do that, when WB had been trying, unsuccessfully, for many, many months, he'd laughed and talked of the differences of *theoretical* and *practical* scientists; the implication being that WB was a 'theoretical' scientist, whilst he was a 'practical' scientist.

Eileen asked Jonathan:

> *Are you a theoretical scientist or a practical scientist?*
> I am a middle of the road scientist.
> *How many are in your group, Jonathan?*
> (Jonathan laughs) Ha, a cast of thousands. There are so many, there is a debate about who's in and who's not. But you know, you have your solid core, you might call them, around you, and they attract others to assist you on your Friday night venture. Yes, the more energy, the merrier it will be.

Jonathan decided it was time to leave but before doing so he gave us the poem below.

*   *   *

> They spend away the eve
> Looking ever hopeful to spirit friends above
> Spirit friends look down
> With appreciation and love

Jonathan finished the session with his blessing:
So I will wish you a mighty happy night, a peaceful night, a God given night. Goodbye my friends.

Chapter 34

Harold

Harold's Message:
Watch for the Energy Changes

It was another physical phenomena sitting. As usual we had the blackout in place. We couldn't see anything in the dark, but as always, there was still much variation with the energies in the room, which, in spite of the darkness, were easily observed. One member commented on how dark it had gone. Paul had slipped into trance and Harold, a new spirit visitor, replied:

The energy does indeed alter the intensity of light and darkness within your room. I would say to you it is more the **changes** that are significant than whether it is dark or light. When you find intensifying darkness, this is a sign of an energy change, which may, under the right circumstances, produce effects. But, equally, when you feel an energy change towards lighter conditions, this also reflects a change in the energy situation within your room. Therefore, you may find that this also can produce effects, of a sort, but it can, nevertheless, produce effects. So it is the **change** you should watch for; rather than extreme darkness or extreme lightness on their own.

And is it at that point, that we are most likely to see something?

Certainly, you will find an intensifying of energy and when you find an intensifying of energy this indeed may provide the ground swell, the watershed, for factors to occur.

Chapter 35

Jacob & Bill

Jacob, who normally takes the sessions for our mediumship development, came through at the end of one of our sittings for physical phenomena. He commented that they (the Spirit Group) had done well that night and had managed to flap Paul's trouser leg. He asked if anyone else had felt anything. One member of the group mentioned that she'd felt energy leaving her. Jacob had rather a unique way of explaining what takes place when the Spirit Group manipulate the energies.

JACOB

Jacob told us:

Yes, well we do take the energies from all of you. It is like those old fashioned bellows you used to get the fire going; if you just put a cork in those bellows, you won't get any air coming through, but if you put a cork in and we all help to compress the bellows, then eventually the pressure will build up to the point were the cork will pop out. You see, it is a bit like that with this physical phenomenon. We must build the energies up; build them up to a certain point; then it all happens (laughing) for a while, and then it doesn't happen any more (laughs) because we have to start building energies up again. You understand me? That's how it works. It is all or nothing with this physical phenomenon.

But you see, my friends, as you become more practiced, as you sit for longer, you will find that the length of time it takes to build up the pressure in the bellows again, is not so long. So this is why, when you go to Stuart's, (reference to physical medium, Stuart Alexander) you see things happen so quickly, one after the other, because each time the bellows are expanded and compressed again it does not take them long to produce new phenomena; so this is how it works.

*   *   *

BILL

Bill talked to us about the energies we send up with our singing. He was asked:

Do you take that energy and use it?
It is like a reservoir of energy, which we try to use in the room for different things. It also helps communication between our worlds. It helps some folk to come through sometime who would have more difficulty coming through otherwise. It also means that we can store some of this energy like a kind of reservoir, which we can then tap into later.

How do you store it?
(Smiling) I believe that's patented information. Davia is saying to me (spirit gate keeper) be mindful, he isn't the only entrepreneur up here.

Does it go out to the world and to the people who ask us for healing?
Yes, we can send some of that energy out to those folk who need it at your beckoning and we are mindful of them at other times too. Yeah we sure are.

Chapter 36

Jonah

The Governing Council in the Spirit World

We couldn't quite understand the name of this spirit guest speaker. He told us:

If you call me Jonah you will not be far wrong. I am not Jonah but my name has some similarity to this word, to this sound.

You are all working hard my friends. We are all working hard also, from our side, but you are working extremely hard. We are gratified by your efforts, most splendid.

Have we done well tonight?
You have done exceedingly, splendidly well.
Are you all any further on then?
Yes, we are moving along nicely; it is a gradual process but we are moving along I assure you. Some of you have felt the energies moving along tonight. Like a tree that grows its seeds; when its seeds are ripe they scatter, they produce the fruit. It has been a good night.
Have you spoken to us before?
No, I have not but I have a keen interest in this aspect of your group's work. We are making our interest felt and known to this place for we are interested in things physical and connecting with things spiritual. We are with you all the time and will work with you to bring things to fruition. We work with your Spirit Group as a kind of counsellor in matters physical, and we bow to their greater knowledge and wisdom, in matters philosophical and to do with wisdom.
Is there a Council in the spirit world?

There are Councils that govern, which have an interest in this form of communication, this form of physical enterprise; the connection with your planet, and therefore, you are known. Groups like yourselves, who set up circles; are known to the Council, are known to those who have oversight of such matters and affairs. Therefore, we send our helpers to try to assist you in your endeavours, for we are concerned to bring about some success to as many groups as we may aid in their development. We wish to role back the frontiers. We wish to roll back the boundaries, the barriers between our two worlds: for the illusion of a barrier is only an illusion; and is therefore, there to be rolled back.

The day before, Paul had heard a voice coming from our computer. The speakers had been left on but the volume knob was on zero. Eileen asked whether Jonah knew anything about it.

Are you aware of who put the noise on the computer?
Yes, this was another experiment to try to influence your electronic machine in order to convey our presence, in order to convey something of what might be achieved. Therefore, we persist; we experiment with different pieces of equipment to discover those we might influence to good effect.
Well you certainly influenced the computer.
Yes, we did, and we shall influence it again.
Were you trying to say something in particular because Paul couldn't hear what you said?
We asked a question, which reflected his interest, yes, but we have much to do; much work still to do.
Were you interested in physical phenomena on the earth plane?
Yes, I was interested.
What sort of a job did you have on the earth plane?
I was a writer of books. My interests extended to those experiments in relation to physical and spiritual. We often do perpetuate our interest beyond the grave, (smiling) the grave that is no grave, so that we may carry on our work and bring it to fruition in another domain.
Do you have any particular advice for us tonight?

We counsel you to carry on. We counsel you to persevere, in patience and harmony. And your patience and harmony will see its fruition.

We know these things take a long time.

You have your signs of activity from time to time, little signs, but out of little signs big signs may grow.

One person in the group thought she'd seen our cone lift earlier. Jonah responded:

Well you may see this occur but it will only be a fraction of movement. We would suggest you put this in a more visible place, but not on your table if you find it too great a distraction. You should do as you do now. You should sing for a time, to raise the energies in harmony with us; for though you cannot hear our voices, it is as if we sing in unison with you, and therefore, this is important. But after a time, you may lower your music and listen and communicate with each other freely, and what may occur will occur.

The same member of the group commented:

I felt as though there was pressure particularly in my upper body and up my arms.

What happens is; as the energy draws near, you have sensed it; you feel the energy in your physical aura.

There was a problem with the mini disc and we lost the next part of the conversation. The sound returned just as Jonah was suggesting; that when we go quietly within, we do it in parallel opposite each other. He was asked:

When you say try it in parallel do you mean two at a time?

Yes two at a time in parallel, opposites to each other. You would do well to ensure as far as possible that you are male, female in your circle as you progress around the circle.

Well my friends I must leave you now but I am glad to have had direct communication with you. I am glad to have the opportunity to meet with you and to know you by name. Therefore, I will be on my way but I am not leaving you. I will be watchful over you and assist your group in whatever way I may.

Chapter 37

Stevenson

Talking about Evidence

One night, when were sitting for physical phenomena, our CD suddenly stopped in the middle of a song. It was quite early in the proceedings and up to that point Paul (the medium) had been singing along with us. We were as usual sitting in the dark; however, it was evident that Paul had been taken back into trance. Shortly after, a spirit, who wanted to be known simply as Stevenson, began to talk to us. His voice sounded urgent and for a few moments, Eileen forgot that the whole purpose of the night was for the Spirit Group to attempt to bring about physical phenomena. She remembers thinking at the time that something very serious must have happened for the spirits to feel they needed to interrupt the session.

Stevenson told us:

> We have need to talk, we have need to talk.
> *What do you want to talk about?*
> You want to bring about some physical phenomena, don't you?
> *That's right.*
> Well, we have done it on you.

Stevenson laughed heartily before continuing:
> We let the wheels of the train come to a stop, by putting the brakes on.

When we'd all finished laughing, our new friend was asked:
Are you part of our Spirit Group now?
No, I am the technical assistant.
Was it you personally who achieved this?
Yes, (laughs again) all hands to the brake; that's what I said.
How did you do it?
Energies can be used to achieve things, to roll them along, or they can be used to block, to pull, to brake. Energies can be used in both of these ways and other ways for that matter, but we are more concerned with the brake potential tonight. So you can adapt these energies to hold things in place or to release them, to move them on, you see. You tend to look to the energies to *move* things, but we can do other things with the right combination.
So the energies are there to use then?
The energies are definitely there to be used as we have demonstrated. We can manipulate your energies and with ours together we can do things, which we would not otherwise be able to do. But you are all free spirits, free givers, so this is most helpful.
Can you tell us a bit about yourself? Do you have a job to do in the spirit world?
I am the 'brake man' (laughs.) I am the technician as I told you before. I have an interest in these matters, an interest in the scientific side of things like your friend WB has. But he was more interested in the theory of science; I am more interested in the practical application; therefore, we complement each other quite well. I do sometimes say to him though; "Oh WB don't fuss and fret over the why of it; it works for goodness sake."

Stevenson laughed heartily again and was asked:

Did you have an interesting scientific bent when you were on this side?
I had a very interesting scientific bent when I was on your side of life, my friend. Like I say though, I was very practically minded. I wanted to make things work, to push, to pull, to invent things you see, that would have some impact, some application. I was not interested in the *why* for itself but more as to *how*. The why could be used to achieve other things, you understand. And I am still of that inclination now, though I have known some others who have switched their

allegiance since entering into the spirit world. They have become interested in the other perspective of things you see. They have exhausted themselves with the practical application of science and they are now interested in the theoretical explanation of science. There are others of course, who have switched the opposite way, to gain a different perspective on life. For even in science, by exploring these different perspectives we grow, we grow as human beings and as spirits, once in the spirit world.

Do you look for groups to work with?

We get the call you see, Michael; we get the call. The call goes out and asks; "Is anyone out there interested; we have a group of experimenters down here and we wish to experiment on them."

One member commented:

My feet went very cold tonight, did that have something to do with what you were doing?

Yes, it has something to do with it. We change the energies in the room to manufacture the best conditions for our purposes. Sometimes it is an *illusion* of cold though, which is created by the energies.

I didn't feel cold apart from my feet.

No, (laughs) it is localised to those who have hot feet that we may make them cold.

Can you turn the CD player back on now that you've made your point?

No, (laughter) I was just about to say to you that we have left you with a predicament, for we have built up the energies nicely to be able to apply the brake but we are now stumped, (laughter) for we have not sufficient energies to release the brake.

This brought about more laughter from the group; Stevenson continued:

So you can try to turn it off and turn it on again, but you may have to change the fuse (laughs.)

Will you be trying other things now?

Yes we will be trying other things on you.

Do the energies have to be mixed by a chemist?

Well, we have to mix and blend the energies certainly, but we would not use the word chemist, as such, though we use a chemist because of his past experience of chemicals on the earth. A chemist and his notion of blending chemicals are not a million miles away but that is as far as this analogy goes.

We hadn't been singing that long tonight when you managed to stop the CD player. Doesn't it take long to build up the energies?

No, the fact that you all come here in like mind already builds up the energies.

Is there anything we can bring into the room that would help you?

No; apart from you all, there is no particular need for anything else. We may experiment with some of the other equipment that these good people possess, at some point.

Note: When Stevenson left we did try to switch the player back on again by simply pressing the on/off button but, as Stevenson had implied, it wouldn't work. We then removed the plug from the socket. After replacing it the player worked OK.

Part 7

General Questions
&
More about the Phoenix Group

Chapter 38

Development Circles & Harmony

Is it a good idea to sit in more than one development circle?

There is no harm in sitting in other circles providing there is some harmony within the different approaches of the leaders of these circles. If you went to one circle and it pursued a particular approach and you went to another and its approach was very different, this could create disharmony in your mind. It could create some conflict in the manner of approach, of the development, but as long as there is a reasonable harmony between the approaches there should be no fear and no reason to be concerned. The harmony within each circle is an important factor also of course. In fact it is one of the *most* important factors and as I have said before, this is a big consideration and is a more important consideration sometimes, than sitting in more than one circle. There needs to be an atmosphere of trust, of positive anticipation and of harmony. These are the important factors.

*   *   *

Someone else asked:

Just before I go to sleep, I get lots of images come into my head. Is this the development of mediumship?

Sometimes, Jane, it is that you are connecting with energies of the spirit world. The time before sleep is a good time to connect with energies, with the spirit world, but you must be careful not to connect with the energies of the spirit world just before you go to sleep so that you enter the sleep period with this connection in place. When you are asleep *it is a time for sleep*, and if you connect with the spirit world just before you go to sleep it could cause you to have a less satisfying sleep, through no fault of your own. It happens because you have opened the channel, the connection, and so you have opened the floodgates.

Another question along similar lines, was asked by another group member:

I find, Hai, when I close my eyes I see pictures and people all the time. It's sometimes just like watching a film. I always thought it was normal and everybody else saw the same sort of thing. Is it just that I'm day-dreaming or is it spirit passing by, that I get a glimpse of?

Hai replied smiling:
Davia is very active tonight. He says be careful who you speak of this to, for men in white coats often come across such stories.

Hai laughed with us for a few moments and then became more serious. He replied:

Yes it is possible, it is very possible to connect with the spirit world in this way, to see many impressions, faces, but you must stay in control of this my friend. *You* must decide when the time is right and when it is not right and you can do as we have recommended before; focus in upon one of these faces or one of these scenes, to see if it is possible to gain a more detailed impression, to connect in a deeper way with the energies.
It's difficult because they go very quickly.
Yes, but focus upon and follow the thread before it disappears.

Hai laughs again and says:
He (Davia) says he will paint them for you so you can see them coming.

Psychic Art

Hai was asked:

> *How does psychic art work?*

It is no different to any other process. It is merely that the image rather than a message is conveyed to the paper. However, it does vary depending upon the artist and upon the connection, for it is not always clear to the artist what the picture will be when it is finished. Sometimes the artist must just let go and go with the flow and the picture will take form, without them knowing for sure what the end result will be.

I heard a psychic artist say once that she did not know what spirit would do and that they just moved her arm.

It is not of course that the spirits move her arm or her hand; rather that they create an impression in her brain that is not fully registered by the brain and which she is not totally conscious of, but they convey an impression to the brain, nevertheless, and the impulses of this impression carry forth signals to her hand.

Transfiguration

A member of our group had been to a transfiguration demonstration and commented that the faces seen on the medium where very similar to the ones seen at an earlier demonstration on the same medium. Hai replied:

Well you know, human expressions are similar the world over. When we try to capture the gesture of someone in particular then it might also seem similar to someone else who used a similar expression, so it is not so easy to give unique detailed portrayals of such people. We can only give an impression, a semblance to what they were like, what they looked like, what their mannerisms were, unless we are able to manifest more concretely using ectoplasm, and therefore, achieve a closer fit to their face.

Referring to the same medium another member commented:

One lady said she could smell an earthy kind of aroma. She asked if it was anything in particular and the medium said that ectoplasm has that kind of smell to it. Do you agree with that, Hai?

Some may pick it up like this, others may pick it up in a different way; however, it has an odour, which may be detected.

Recurring Dreams

A young woman gave Hai some personal information about a recurring dream. She wondered if it was a memory of a previous life. Hai replied:

Well you may find that this indeed is a memory of a previous life; this may be possible. It may also be possible that you have travelled while you have been asleep and are remembering the conditions and surroundings that you've encountered. Once the mind has latched on to an image, a dream sequence may repeat the sequence ad-nauseam when the mind is asleep. So it is hard to disentangle what may be occurring here. It may be a past life or it may be a dream or it may be a visit while you have been dreaming, but possibly the sequence of the dream has been repeated because of its unusual nature which the mind has latched onto and repeated on other occasions.

Our Contract with the Spirit World

Hai has always emphasised that we should view him and the rest of the Spirit Group, simply as friends who are doing a job together. One lady wanted to know whether we agreed to work with spirit before coming to this life. She asked:

Is the plan to work with spirit made before we come to earth?

Sometimes the pact is made before you start your life on the earth. Sometimes the pact is already sealed, so when you come to your life on the earth it is simply a matter of time before you take up your work. However, it is a partnership, a partnership of friends as I have emphasized in the past and you should view it in this way, as friends, joining you to spend some time together, to work together, and to share the moment together. This is important. It helps the harmony to view us in this way; therefore, this is the way that we should be viewed. We should not be viewed as strange, as alien, and as different to you. You must just treat us as one of you.

Chapter 39

More about the Phoenix Group

Some Light Hearted Fun

To finish this book, we thought our readers may like to hear a little more of the more personal side of some of the spirits who join us at our sittings and in particular the humour that comes over on a regular basis. This, in some ways, has been the most difficult part of the book. Over the years we have become so familiar with these energies that we have come to love them like our own family. Therefore, we need to mention here, that if we have said more about one than another, it is simply that we have more information perhaps, and therefore, more *to* say about that particular spirit. We find it hard to describe the love we feel for our Spirit Group and each time any one of them comes to talk to us we feel *their* deep love for us. It would be impossible to have favourites. We love them all equally.

Hai

Hai is affectionately referred to as 'Old Hai' by the rest of the Spirit Group and was a Buddhist Abbot when he last lived on the earth plane in China around 800 AD. He is the leader of the Phoenix Group and is clearly an evolved soul though he would not describe himself in that way. Hai has indicated that his reason for communicating with us is to pass on wisdom and teaching. At times he can appear serious, stern even, but at others he will show that he has a keen sense of humour.

When last on the earth plane, Hai was well known for his use of stories to demonstrate a point. Hai still loves to tell stories. Below is a story (told with humour) that he used to answer a question about **enlightenment**. He began:

I tell you a story:

A monk asks his Abbott what he has to do to gain enlightenment and the Abbott asks the monk,

"Have you had breakfast, my friend?" The monk says, yes, thinking—what has this got to do with enlightenment. The Abbott then said to him, "Then go and wash your dishes—end of lesson."

Hai continued:

So this seems simple, but the **Truth** is simple: There is a Harmony, it is One Reality, which embraces everything; **there is not a hairs breadth of difference.**

On another occasion, Eileen told Hai, that a friend who had developed a skill in psychic drawing, had asked to be allowed to come to the next sitting because he wanted to try to 'pick him up' (he wanted to receive his image and draw it.)

Hai responded smiling:

It has been a long time since someone attempted to pick me up, or to draw me for that matter. There were those who came to the monastery to draw me, and they wanted me to sit still for some time. This is no great problem to a Buddhist meditation monk.

WB

WB, our spirit scientist, works with the energies of the group during our sittings. He was also a scientist when last on the earth plane, and tells us he lived in Edinburgh around the 1800's. We understand that WB's first name is William; however, he is apparently, familiar with the term WB so prefers to continue with this now. When he first communicated, WB seemed quite formal indicating that he usually preferred to stay in the background. Nevertheless, over time, he shared with us something of his life on earth and we began to feel his warmth and glimpse his 'lighter' side. WB told us that he had concentrated on his research to the detriment of many other things; consequently he never married.

On his return to the spirit world he reflected on his life and realised that a relationship with the opposite sex could have enriched his life. However, true to all happy endings, WB told us that he's now met someone in the spirit world whom he shares his life with; her name is Sylvia. When he communicates now, we always ask about Sylvia, and WB assures us that she is well and they are still together.

The following communication took place just before Christmas. Eileen asked if Sylvia was well. After confirming that she was, WB had the following to say about Christmas.

He told us:
I enjoy this time of year for although we do not celebrate in exactly the same way as yourselves, we do partake of your festivities and enjoy them. I enjoy them because it was a time when it was not of particular pleasure for me when on the earth plane. But now I have the company of a delightful female soul, I am able to partake much more in the enjoyment of the season. Yes, to make up for some lost ground, if you like.

Well my friends, I will move on and I wish you the blessings of the season.

Just prior to this book being published, WB paid us one of his rare visits. Eileen asked him whether he could offer some advice, for the book, about the development of mediumship. We've transcribed WB's thoughts on the matter, below:

Well, I would say to people, that you should be steadfast. It is no easy process, this development, and no easy task at all. Therefore, it is important to be steadfast and resolute but also calm with it. It is no use getting into a frenzy over it. You should just merely walk the path, like you walk on a little journey. You should put one foot in front of the other and as sure as anything you will get to your destination. So it is important to learn this discipline, but with a calm heart and mind; that is most important.

Davia

It was hard to decide where to start when attempting to describe Davia and his humour and we've already said a little at the front of this book. Davia tells us he lived in the deep jungle of Papua New Guinea some three or four hundred years ago (give or take a hundred years, he says.) He had many wives and it has become something of a game, with the regular members of our Home Circle, to try to elicit just how many wives he had. Davia often tells us stories about the antics he got up to when they had canoe races between other villages and how he used to take the honey from the bees nests. Some of our 'guest speakers' often refer to the 'paddle' they say he carries about with him in the spirit land and to the bone he displays through his nose.

Davia's role seems to be that of stage manager/gatekeeper, though he prefers the title 'keeper of the gate' because he says it sounds grander. He seeks out those spirits whom he feels have some wisdom to offer which they've got from their experiences during one of their lives. Some seem to 'apply' to come through whilst others seem to receive—an ever so slight—push. It would appear, that Davia manages the whole 'cast' of spirit visitors (no wonder he refers to himself as 'stage manager.' Our spirit friends tell us, that when it is time for them to go he simply raises his 'paddle' and gives them a beautiful smile *with his eyes*. One night Davia was asked why he carried a paddle:

Why do you carry a paddle?
It is my *insignia* like your Roman General (referring to a recent guest speaker.) *I'm* not pretentious though, so I carry a paddle.
Couldn't you have chosen a smaller trinket?
Well it is not so big you know. It is not like one of those big oars that Maximus' (Roman General) galley slaves used to use. Not that big but big enough for the purpose, fit for the intent (laughs heartily.)
Did you carve that when you were on the earth plane?
Well, I sort of, got it from someone else, who carved it for me.
Oh right, you—sort of—got it?
Yes.
Did you win it in a race?
No, no, no. He was kind enough to donate it to me.

We thought the following communication would provide you with another sample of the spirit energy we call Davia. One night, as the end of the session drew close, WB indicated that he could hear Davia coming to close the proceedings. Someone asked what he meant.

WB replied:

It is like; oh how can I describe it—it is like the Jack and the Beanstalk story. You know; Jack is in the giant's house and he is sat quietly hiding in some corner and all of a sudden he hears the giant returning home (the medium thumps a couple of times on the arm of the chair) this is like Davia coming from afar. I would say he lacks finesse, you know. And yet, in another sense of the word, he is the best person at finessing that I have ever come across. Do you follow me? I would not have wished to play cards with him, not on my bad days.

When we'd finished laughing he continued:

Well my friends, I think I will have to leave you because the giant's footsteps are approaching, but I will promise you I will make sure that I will not leave it so long next time. So from both myself, and Sylvia, we wish you a pleasant conclusion to your evening, and pleasant refreshment (laughs) on your return to the lower realms (referring to our room downstairs) only a pun you understand. We will move on to make way for the great one (again referring to Davia.)

Jacob

We explained earlier that Jacob is not one of the original members of the Phoenix group but was 'co-opted on' later. One night a member of the group asked:

Have you become a member of the Phoenix group now, Jacob?

Yes, well I am certainly in and out, but a lot more *in* these days. I am on the periphery but not on the periphery, if you follow my meaning. I am quite involved yes, since they drafted me in, since they experimented with all those other people, those poor people whom they sent on their way. (Jacob was referring to the many other spirits whom the Spirit Group had sent to us to 'try out' before they settled on Jacob)

Jacob laughed and added:
That's not nice, is it?

He laughed again and continued, 'tongue in cheek:'

When you think about it, we're supposed to be all loving up here, all embracing, but they did not measure up to the task (much more laughter.) No, but they have found other useful things to do. It is a matter of getting the right connection, between you and us, as a group, so it's just finding the right fit, the right key to turn the lock, the right affinity, the right harmony; all these things. So, (smiling) it is not *really*, like we have dismissed them to the outer wastelands or anything. They will have found their own valuable role to play elsewhere. Nobody is wasted here.

This is unlike your world I think, for there are many in your society whose talents are wasted and neglected. (Jacob became serious) This is very sad to us and no one takes the trouble to find out what they can contribute, how they can help, what we can learn from them, and what skills they possess and can apply. This is not done all the time in your world and this is a great sadness to us because it undermines the value and shows a lack of valuing of the individual person. But this never happens on our plane. We value everyone and we try to find the best way that they may help and are happy with.

When last on the earth plane, Jacob, of Jewish faith, was a watchmaker living in Poland. At the end of one of our sessions just before Christmas time, Jacob finished with the following blessing:

I hope you all have a very happy Christmas. I did not celebrate Christmas when I was on your earth plane because I was of the Jewish religion but I wish you a happy Christmas. When we come to this plane (spirit world) we understand that the *occasion* of the festivities is not important, but that the festivities themselves *are* important because it brings people together in joy and happiness. This is what is important, so we share the enjoyment through *your* festivities whether it is your festivities at Christmas time or the festivities of the Buddhists or other religions.

Someone commented:
You must be very busy then in the spirit world.

Jacob smiled and replied:

We do the rounds. This is enjoyable and because we are not shackled any longer with those thoughts; "Ah Christian tradition and we have Christmas, or Buddhist tradition for Buddha holiday;" we have a good time all year round you see. It is a pity people do not realise this and they could take a bit of every religion, and they could have a good time all year round. So, my friends, I shall go and wish you 'all the best.' That is what you say isn't it?—All the best of everything to you. Goodbye.

Thomas

You will find one of Thomas' communications earlier in this book, with some information about his last life on earth. You can also read more about him on our website. However, on a recent visit, Thomas was asked if he would like to say anything about this book. He obliged with the following:

Well ma'm, all I would say, is that people have got to use the book like a little light and they've got to keep exploring by using that light as a starting point. They've got to explore for themselves and if they keep looking into things they will find their knowledge, understanding and ability will grow. They've just got to persevere, go at it, calm like, with patience; knowing it's real—and there are no doubts about that—it is real; but they should just calmly pursue communication and link to us, as and when they can.

Isleen

Isleen has been with the Phoenix Group since its inception and she was the spirit who first worked with Paul when he was sitting for trance. Hai only took over when they were sure that Paul would be able to cope with his energy. We were told later that Isleen had been chosen for the job because of her gentle energy, which was thought to be useful, particularly in the early stages, in helping Paul feel safe.

In those early days, when Eileen and Paul sat alone, Isleen's role developed further. At some stage during each sitting she would come through and reassure Eileen that the trance was developing normally and would explain what they had been doing (or trying to do) that night.

Later, when our Home Circle was developed, Isleen's role changed again as she developed our meditation sessions which was also the start of the development groups. There is much banter during our meditation nights, from Davia, as he teases Isleen about her softly spoken voice. However, it is abundantly clear that all the banter is said with much love and that Davia holds her in high esteem.

Isleen told us she last lived on the earth plane in the 1800s. She came from an Irish family and lived on a farm in Ireland. She had mediumship abilities when on the earth plane and continues to act as a medium now between the different spirit realms. When communication first began, Isleen told us that she was no longer with her husband in the spirit world. At that point it didn't occur to us to ask if she had found another partner. It was only during the course of one of our recent conversations that we discovered that Isleen has, what she described as her 'beau,' whom, it would seem; she has been with for some considerable time.

Carol

Carol also has been with the Phoenix group since its formation; however, she does not take a direct role in our circle meetings. We are told that she prefers to stay in the background and 'do her bit' and we have no doubt that, though we rarely talk to her, she makes a valuable contribution to the enterprise. In one of her few communications, which you will find earlier in this book, Carol explains how she is always connected to us.

Carol was the daughter of a wealthy family during Roman times. It would appear that she's had other lives since but chooses to communicate with the personality she had in Roman times because of a link we have with her from those times. One night Eileen asked Hai what Carol's role was within the group. We thought his reply was fitting to end this book.

"Carol lends us her energy, her vibration, her lovingness. She is a rock of love, power, and compassion, of emotion. She does this because of the bonds from past times, (lives) so she commits herself to this enterprise in love, especially for you and Paul and past associations. Therefore, she gives her energies and devotion to this enterprise.

You are already aware that she knew you both in Roman times. You have both had a special relationship with her; therefore, there is a bond of love between you all. And Carol is another example of what I have spoken to you all of on many occasions: The bond of love is everlasting, eternal, cannot be broken, endures and perseveres through the ages, through time—which is of no account to this bond for it endures, it is timeless, it is eternal. And so, Carol is exemplar of this; she manifests this that I have spoken of many times."

About the Authors

After training in the social sciences Paul McGlone embarked on a career in community work. He subsequently moved into Education and Training and had a long career as a Lecturer in the Caring Services. He now has a private hypnotherapy practice. Paul has had a long-standing interest in all religions and sees communication with the spirit world as contributing to the pursuit of Spiritual Truth.

Communications through Paul's trance mediumship are regularly published on his web site. Paul's trance work has prompted a new interest in writing and a number of publications are in preparation, including a novel based on the themes of the spirit communications.

Eileen McGlone worked for over twenty-five years in a Local Authority Social Services Department, as a Social Worker and Team Manager. She became interested in Spiritual Healing in 1981 after she'd received her first healing treatment.
Some time later she received training in Spiritual Healing and Reiki. Eileen now works from home. She practices and teaches Reiki, compiles manuscripts of spirit communication and facilitates the meditation and development sessions held at Paul and Eileen's home.

The authors can be contacted at
Tranquil Spirit
339 Bramhall Lane
Stockport
Cheshire
SK3 8TP
England
0161 483 7014
www.tranquilspirit.info
Email: info@tranquilspirit.info

978-0-595-37989-7
0-595-37989-3

Made in the USA
Lexington, KY
11 August 2015